if you're

clueless

about

selling
your house

and
want to
know more

if you're

clueless

about

selling

your house

and

want to

know more

DEARBORN™
A **Kaplan Professional** Company

If You're Clueless about Selling Your House and Want to Know More

Series Creator: Seth Godin
Acquisitions Editor: Jean Iversen
Managing Editor: Jack Kiburz
Interior and Cover Design: Karen Engelmann
Typesetting: Omega Publishing Services, Inc.

Published by Dearborn, a Kaplan Professional Company

Printed in the United States of America

99 00 01 10 9 8 7 6 5 4 3 2 1

Library of Congress Cataloging-in-Publication Data

Sparks, Bonnie.
    If you're clueless about selling your house and want to know more
    / Bonnie Sparks.
        p.   cm.
    Includes bibliographical references and index.
    ISBN 0-7931-3119-7 (paper)
    1. Real estate agents.   2. House selling.   3. House selling-
-United States.   4. Real estate business–United States.   I. Title.
HD255.S693 1999
333.33'83–dc21   99-12034
                                                            CIP

Dearborn books are available at special quantity discounts to use as premiums and sales promotions, or for use in corporate training programs. For more information, please call the Special Sales Manager at 800-621-9621, ext. 4514, or write to Dearborn Financial Publishing, Inc., 155 North Wacker Drive, Chicago, IL 60606-1719.

Other Clueless Books

If You're Clueless about Mutual Funds and Want to Know More

If You're Clueless about Retirement Planning and Want to Know More

If You're Clueless about Saving Money and Want to Know More

If You're Clueless about the Stock Market and Want to Know More

If You're Clueless about Insurance and Want to Know More

If You're Clueless about Starting Your Own Business and
Want to Know More

If You're Clueless about Accounting and Finance and Want to Know More

If You're Clueless about Getting a Great Job and Want to Know More

If You're Clueless about Selling and Want to Know More

If You're Clueless about Financial Planning and Want to Know More

If You're Clueless about Buying a Home and Want to Know More

Acknowledgments

Like the sale of a home, this book required teamwork from a variety of professionals. I would especially like to thank Karen Watts for her patience and perseverance in the completion of this project and Lark Productions for their confidence in my writing ability. I'm grateful, too, for Laura Spinale's keen editorial eye.

Kay and Robert Kent were instrumental in some of the creative content and I am most appreciative. Ron Reem provided insights on inspections that I found to be valuable.

The Steinbrech Agency provided the legwork and support necessary to meet recurring deadlines and they will forever have my gratitude.

The California Association of REALTORS® was very generous in allowing me the use of their association forms to clarify concepts and terminology raised in the text. I am so grateful for such generosity.

My special thanks to Carla Cross, friend and colleague, who recommended me to author the book. I have grown immensely as a result of the opportunity.

Contents

GETTING *a clue* about *Selling* YOUR HOUSE

CHAPTER ONE

You want to sell your house. Terrific! This book will help you do that.

All you have to do is decide whether to hire a broker or go the FSBO (for sale by owner) route (making sure to assemble a consulting "dream team"), prepare the property for showings, set a competitive price, market your house, sign disclosures, find your best buyer, negotiate and counteroffer, close and move.

You have no idea what any of this means, do you? Get a clue. Read this book and you'll learn

- How to choose a real estate agent

- What to do if your want to sell your house yourself (commonly referred to in the trade as an FSBO, or "for sale by owner")

1

- Your legal rights and obligations as a homeseller

- How to market your house

- How to price your house

- How to prepare your house so that it looks good when being toured by a stampede of potential buyers

- Strategies for negotiating less-than-stellar offers

- What you'll need to do after negotiating a deal but before closing on the property

- How to determine the tax bite on homeselling profits

First things first, though. Let's talk about why you even want to move.

Selling: The Big "Should I?"

Once, long, long ago, you fell in love with your house. Admit it. Sure, you read all the books that told you to buy with your head, not your heart. But unless you're a professional real estate investor, you felt a spark. Maybe it was only an infatuation. Maybe it matured into true love.

You coveted the place so much that you applied for a loan, paid for inspections, committed to a mortgage, waded through the paperwork of closing, footed the bill for closing costs, and, oh yeah, scraped together the bucks for a down payment. Then you probably spent a chunk of change redecorating.

Now you want to do it all again. Why?

Here are some likely reasons:

- *A better location.* You want to move to a neighborhood that has a greater sense of community, less noise, a lower crime rate, better schools, or easier access to shopping and other activities.

- *Space.* As the family grows, you need a bigger house. As the kids leave home, you want a cozier abode.

- *Finances.* You've just garnered a huge promotion—making megabucks—and you deserve a dream home to go with your dream job. Conversely, you just suffered a layoff and need to reassess your lifestyle, perhaps moving into a smaller home (read smaller mortgage and lower upkeep costs) or an apartment.

- *Job change.* Your company has transferred you to another city and you need to move.

- *Your spouse died.* You may find yourself unable to bear living in a house built for two.

- *Divorce.* It's time for a fresh start.

- *There's something structurally wrong.* You need to move before the roof caves in.

Do You Wanna or Do You Hafta?

Before you start ringing up real estate agents, decide whether you actually *need* to sell or whether you just *want* to.

If you need to sell, put the place on the market. If you just want to move, hold out for the strongest sales arena possible. This means waiting until area property prices either stabilize or peak.

Looking for a new neighborhood? Consider the following scenarios.

STRUCTURAL DEFECTS

You may want to move by a month from Thursday, the expiration date on your rickety roof. You'd fix the roof if you could, but you don't have the cash. And you have too little invested in the place to get a loan based on your equity in it.

So you put the house on the market. If you're in the situation described above, this is quite possibly the soundest decision you can make.

Remember though, you are required by law to disclose to would-be buyers any known structural defects in the house (see chapter 4). Your buyer will demand that you lower the price of your house to accommodate necessary repairs.

You can still sell the house. Unfortunately, you're unlikely to get what you want for it.

Oh Good Heavens, We've Moved To Amityville!

People sometimes decide to sell when they learn, after moving in, that their new house has been "psychologically impacted" or "stigmatized." This means that a murder, suicide, or other traumatic event has taken place there. Some people just can't live in a house with such bad vibes.

If you're one of those people, you have several choices. You can sell the place. You can rent it out. You can also attempt to remove the vibe from the house. This is a religious or spiritual effort to clean the place up, and you'd need to consult a religious adviser. It's a little out there, but it seems to have worked for some who were willing to try it.

Henry and Pearl, both in their early 60s, bought their house 32 years ago. For a long time they enjoyed a great house in a great neighborhood. Now, though, the area suffers from an escalating crime rate. Vandals have damaged their house. Pearl worries about staying home alone while Henry works.

Now let's look at Jane. A busy single mother, she'd like to live closer to her town's central shopping district.

Clearly, Henry and Pearl need to move. Their peace of mind is at stake. Jane, however, wants to relocate for convenience's sake. She should consider whether proximity to nearby shopping is worth the effort and expense of selling.

Let's look at your reasons for selling, and determine whether they're "needs" or "wants."

Space. If you plan to buy up, do you actually need more space because of a growing family or a newly launched home business? Or do you and your spouse simply each want a private den? If you've chosen to downsize, consider whether finances require the move, or if you've just grown tired rattling around a big house now that the kids are grown.

Finances. Laid off, looking at a long unemployment haul, you may face the unpleasant choice of selling your house or being foreclosed upon. You need to get out of your mortgage payments. Promoted, at the top of your game, you just want a house with more panache.

Job. If you've been transferred from Montana to Missouri, and you're unwilling to deal with the hassle of acting as a long-distance landlord, you have to sell your house.

Your spouse died. Closure may prove impossible if you continue to live in a house haunted by the memories of your spouse. You may need to move to get on with your life.

Divorce. The end of a marriage often entails the sale of a house.

What Do You Want from Your New Place?

After analyzing your reasons for selling your house, think about what you want from your new neighborhood and your new home; then take steps to make sure you get what you want.

Location. If you want a peaceful atmosphere, relatively crime- and noise-free, consider moving into a gated, deed-restricted community. (Deed restrictions regulate homeowners' conduct. The restrictions can limit everything from the color you paint your house to the pets you can own to the hours you are allowed to play your opera.) If you want a better education for the kids, call up the school board in the area you've targeted and ask for district-wide results of standardized tests.

Space. Some people who say they want a bigger house really want more privacy. The family of four wants a place where Josh can play his Nintendo games full blast, where Susie can practice her ballet, and where mom and dad can watch PBS in peace. Since all these activities involve noise, this family should consider a stand-alone home, one in which they can get as loud as they like without disturbing each other or the neighbors.

Conversely, a lot of sellers say they want a smaller house when really what they want is less responsibility. Consider a co-op or a condo development, one where a home-owners association tends the grounds and makes necessary external repairs.

SOURCES OF ADVICE

If you're trying to decide whether to sell, besides speaking to a real estate agent, don't hesitate to contact your:

- Lender

- Certified Public Accountant

- Attorney

- Insurance Agent

Discuss the alternatives available to you. You may have to pay for consultations, but it will be money well spent. Time spent with the pros will help you decide whether to put your house on the market.

Finances. You may sell your house to bring in some cash to pay off other debts, and that's fine. Just make sure that you are going to walk away from the deal with enough money to do so.

If you're selling your house because you're making more money and like the prestige of a new home, consider whether you want to buy the largest house available in your current neighborhood or whether you want to go for a more modest home in the classiest area of town.

Job. Use your transfer as the perfect excuse to get out of a house or neighborhood you may have tired of and into a place that fulfills your dreams.

Your spouse died. Consider whether a move will actually ease the pain and loneliness and provide you with surroundings in which you feel comfortable. Many widows and widowers find it better to face their loss on their home turf, and only then decide whether to move.

Divorce. Your ex was the one who wanted the six-bedroom farmhouse in the exact middle of nowhere. You always coveted a condo in town. Now's the time to go for it.

Alternatives to Selling

Newton wrote that for every action there is an equal but opposite reaction. Homesellers should know that every reason to sell can be countered with a reason to stay. If you've decided to stay put, consider what you can do to improve your home life.

Here are some options.

- *Improve your neighborhood.* Want a quieter, friendlier block? Think about actually getting to know your neighbors. Knock on doors, just to say hi. Organize a neighborhood get-together or block party, to give people a chance to mingle. If crime rates have escalated, contact the local police department about organizing a neighborhood watch program.

- *Make your own convenience.* If you're tired of running across town every time you need to buy some hamburger meat, buy food in bulk and freeze it. If you're trekking 10 miles to the high school every night to pick up Jimmie after football practice, organize a car pool with some other football moms.

- *Grow your home.* Need more space? Consider adding a room or two onto your current abode. Remember though, you will likely not recoup the entire cost of construction if you do eventually decide to sell.

- *Go ahead, be irresponsible!* If you wanted to move to a condo or co-op because you've grown sick of mowing the lawn, cleaning your own pool, or painting the house, stay where you are and hire people to do these chores for you. Remember, paying a gardener, pool guy, and painter will probably cost less than the monthly fee on your condo over the lifetime of your ownership.

- *Get the monkey off your back.* If you feel strangled by mounting debts, you may be able to find a way to put your financial house in order without selling your bricks-and-mortar home. Work with your lender on a refinancing program or a second mortgage; apply for a home equity loan; or even rent a room or two to bring in some extra cash.

- *Redecorate.* If your spouse recently died, you may feel more comfortable in the house you once shared if you redecorate and set aside painful reminders.

- *Talk to your ex.* If you truly love your house, buy out your ex.

Remember, Selling Means You Have to Move

Before placing your house on the market, make sure there are houses out there you like better than your current digs. Otherwise, you may end up like Ben and Emily.

Ben and Emily didn't start looking for a new place until they got an offer on their current house. Days and weeks passed and—you guessed it—they failed to find a house that they like as well as the house they had put up for sale.

In the meantime, the buyer had shelled out some cash for a loan application and closing costs. Upon learning that Ben and Emily had decided to take their house off the market, the buyer got royally, and understandably, ticked off. The buyer demanded, and received, a refund of the earnest money. Ben and Emily were just thankful that the buyer didn't sue to recoup other expenses. (The legal ramifications of backing out of a sale vary from place to place. Talk with a qualified lawyer.)

Timing Is Everything

If you *need* to place your house on the market, do it now. If you only *want* to sell, consider waiting for the best market possible.

Selling in a Depressed Market

A depressed market is also often called a *buyer's market.* This is an economic condition in which you'll find more properties on the block than prospects out looking.

If a buyer's market prevails in your area, sell only if you absolutely have to. And prepare yourself for a long wait. To speed up the process a bit, consider dropping the price of your house as low as possible, and offer the buyer perks such as new carpeting or a fresh paint job. Get creative. You may even consider leaving your mint '57 Chevy Impala in the garage. Okay, maybe not, but you get the point.

Selling in a Strong Market

A strong local economy often leads to a *seller's market*, or a situation in which you have throngs of buyers competing for a small pool of available houses.

It's a good time to move, if you have to. What the hey—this is a good time to move even if you just feel like it.

Spurred by a strong seller's market, you may be tempted to get aggressive in your asking price. Resist the temptation. Pricing your house too high may mean a long wait to sell, even in the best economy.

Other Timing Considerations

Convertible car sales jump in the summer when everyone envisions taking to the open road, the wind blowing through their hair. Similarly, some months are just better for selling houses than others.

- *Late March through June.* Terrific months for selling. It's warm enough for people to get out and house hunt. And some will want to be settled in their new digs well before the kids start a new school year.

- *February through mid–March.* In warmer climates (such as Florida) these are great months to sell to people looking for retirement properties or second homes. Conversely, they can prove very slow months in colder climates.

- *The Holiday Season.* Forget the myth that it's impossible to sell a house during this time. While you may find fewer buyers knocking on your door between Thanksgiving and New Year's Day, those who do show up are serious buyers. Which means that you won't experience too much inconvenience having to clean up your place for the "we're just looking" crowd, and you'll garner a good price from serious buyers.

- *July through August.* Vacations take up potential buyers' time, so these are slow months.

- *September through November.* These months also can be slow. Unless a job transfer uproots a family and forces it to house hunt after school starts in the fall, you mostly find people hunkering down in the fall.

There's a caveat to all this: A market will tilt to the seller's advantage whenever the economy and interest rates are good—whatever the month of the year.

Organize

Realistically, it will take a minimum of 90 days to sell and close on your house. That's in a strong market and if you get an acceptable offer within the first weeks your house is on the market. In a weaker market, expect a much longer wait.

There's lots of work to be done just preparing to put your house on the block. You'll learn all about it later in this book. For now, though, have a look at this time line, so you know which chores to complete when.

Week 1: Prepare house. Put it on the market.

Week 2: Begin advertising campaign.

Weeks 3 and 4: Show house to buyers. Continue marketing campaign.

Week 5: Buyer makes offer. Negotiate. Continue advertising house.

Week 6: Sign contract with buyer.

Weeks 7 and 8: Buyer applies for financing. House is appraised.

Week 9: Begin house repairs. Prepare for closing.

Weeks 10–11: Repairs are completed. Close the deal. Move.

Bottom-Line Thinking

By taking the time to read this chapter, you've begun the homeselling process.

You should now have a clue about:

- Whether you need to move or only want to move

- What you hope to achieve by selling your house

- Alternatives to selling

- The best months to sell

- A sales schedule

TO LEARN MORE

To find out more about your local market and its current conditions, call a reputable real estate agent or take a field trip to your county courthouse. Find out how many homes have sold recently, their prices, and their locations. The more information you have about your local market, the better able you'll be to determine whether this is the right time to sell.

THE *Right* AGENT

CHAPTER TWO

So you're officially selling your house? Good for you! But how do you place your house on the market? Bellowing through a megaphone has crossed your mind but you figure there has to be a better way to do it.

You may want to hire a real estate agent to help you market your property, show it, and guide you through negotiations and closing. Choosing an agent can be a tricky business. Like all professions, the real estate field boasts a number of extremely competent workers, with a few quacks and charlatans thrown in for bad measure.

Read this chapter and you'll learn how to choose the right real estate agent. You'll get a clue about:

- How the real estate business works

- Which companies to contact

- Which agents to interview

- Which questions to ask

- How to check references

- What forms you need to sign to bind your relationship with your agent

- How you want your house represented in the marketplace

- How your agent makes his or her money

People considering selling their houses on their own will find guidelines in chapter 3.

How Does It Work?

To choose the best real estate agent, you should know a little about how the real estate business works.

The professionals who'll help sell your house are called *brokers* and *agents*—in other words, salespeople. Both are licensed by the state. Brokers always undergo more rigorous training and testing than sales agents. That's because the broker supervises all agents working on behalf of the real estate, or brokerage, firm. You are essentially the broker's client, although the bulk of your interactions may be with one of the broker's associates—the agent.

Legally, the broker and any salespeople in the firm must:

- *Protect your confidentiality.* When negotiating a sale, the broker and the agent must keep confidential any information that may lessen your bargaining position. You will probably discuss with your agent your reasons for selling your house. You may say things such as, "We have to get out, the mortgage payments are killing us," or "Harry's circulation is really bad these days, and the winters are wearing him out. We need to be out of this house and settled into a warmer climate by October." These revelations indicate an urgency on your part. If the buyer knew of this

The Broker-Agent or Broker-Associate

We've told you that two categories of real estate professionals will help you sell your house—brokers and agents. We lied.

There are really three categories. Brokers, agents, and broker-agents or broker-associates.

Who are these people?

They are real estate professionals who hold a broker's license but have decided to simply sell rather than to operate their own agencies.

Some terrific real estate agents go through the difficult broker's licensing process because they like the prestige of the word *broker* next to their names. They wouldn't dream of actually opening their own agencies because they make a lot more money selling than they would running an office.

If you should meet a broker-agent or broker-associate, take notice. The fact that this professional went out of the way to secure a broker's license usually indicates a very strong career focus.

urgency, he or she might come in with a lowball offer. That's why your broker or salesperson may not reveal this type of information to anyone.

- *Obey your (lawful) instructions.* The key word here is *lawful*. Here's an example. Your real estate agent or broker will likely help you determine the asking price of your house. But in the end, you decide what to sell it for. Say you've decided to set the price at $120,000. Even if the agent believes it would sell faster at $118,000, he or she must market it at your

price. (You may decide to lower your asking price, of course, if the house sits on the market for a long time with nary a nibble.) However, your buyer does not have to follow any instructions that might prove illegal. Say you know that your roof is likely to cave in next Thursday. Laws demand that you disclose such a defect to potential buyers. You can't tell your broker or agent, "Keep quiet about the roof. We'll get a better price if the buyer doesn't know."

- *Keep an accounting of the cash flow.* The broker has to provide you with a report of any money (such as earnest money) or property that comes into his or her possession on your behalf during the transaction.

- *Demonstrate loyalty.* The broker and the agent need to be loyal to you, as their client, even when it means putting your interests before their own. Here's an example. The broker and salesperson make their money from selling your house. The amount they earn is a percentage of the sales price. This is called a *commission.* You may have decided to list your house for $150,000, but you're willing to accept an offer of $135,000 because you want a quick sale. The broker cannot insist that you hold out for the list price simply to increase the commission.

- *Provide disclosure.* Your broker or sales agent must tell you any information that could affect the marketing and sale of your house. Suppose a potential buyer offers you $160,000 for a $180,000 house. If the buyers

SELLER'S DISCLOSURE

Most states mandate that homeowners complete a Seller's Disclosure of Property Condition Form (see Appendix D) before signing a listing contract. This form alerts your agent and potential buyers to any serious flaws in your house, such as a bad roof, a shoddy electrical system, and so forth.

If your house was built before 1978, you will also have to sign a Lead-Based Paint Disclosure Form (see Appendix B), alerting the public to any lead-based paint in the home. As you may know, children have become sick from eating paint chips that contain lead.

These disclosures are discussed more thoroughly in chapter 4.

have said to your broker, "Well, we're coming in with a lowball offer, but we'll probably go up to $175,000," your broker must reveal this information to you.

State real estate laws usually demand that brokers provide care, skill, and diligence in the performance of their duties, but many brokers don't actually go out and show properties. They spend the bulk of their time running the firm and supervising their salespeople.

You'll spend most of your time with an agent, but you must get to know the broker. And here's why.

Let's say you have a cousin in the business, an agent with a sound reputation. Call her Sylvia. You want Sylvia to market and sell your house. Be aware of this, though: Any contracts that you sign for representation of your house are written between you and the brokerage firm, with only a line or two noting that Sylvia will serve as the company's representative.

"No problem," you think, "as long as Sylvia is our primary contact. We know we can trust her." In most cases you're probably right; there shouldn't be a problem.

Suppose, though, that Sylvia decides to change companies after you've signed the contract but before you've sold your house. The right to sell the house—also known as a *listing*—doesn't go with Sylvia. It stays with the company she has just quit. So, unless Sylvia's old broker agrees to cancel your listing so you can take it to Sylvia's new firm, you're on the hook and you will likely be assigned a new representative from the firm.

Trade Associations, and Why You Should Care

Many brokers and salespersons belong to one of two national trade associations: the National Association of Realtors or the National Association of Real Estate Brokers. Members of the National Association of Realtors are called REALTORS® or Realtor-Associates®. Members of the National Association of Real Estate Brokers are called Realtists.

You may want to hire a broker who belongs to one of these organizations for the following reasons:

- *Code of ethics.* Salespersons who are either REALTORS® or Realtists subscribe to a very high code of ethics. Those who do not belong to these groups are bound only by the standards mandated by the licensing organization in your state.

- *Multiple Listing Service (MLS).* As discussed later in this book, it is likely that one agent will market and try to sell your house but another agent—one representing a different brokerage firm completely—might actually bring in the buyers. This situation can come about through a multiple listing service (MLS)—a computerized database of all the properties available for sale in a given area. This database is managed and run by local Boards of Realtors. Only REALTORS® can access this information. You might choose to employ a REALTOR® so that all the other agents in your area have access to information about your house and are able to match it to a likely buyer.

- *Continuing education.* Both these professional organizations offer continuing education opportunities to their members. If your agent has taken advantage of these, you know that he or she is career-oriented and works hard to stay abreast of the latest changes in the field.

Types of Brokers

You should interview several brokers and agents to determine which one you want to represent you in the sale of your house. Contract only with someone who embraces sound business practices and has a sound track record. You also want an agent that you can get along with. If you already know an agent you like, you may want your primary interview to be with him or her, along with a quick meeting with the broker to make sure the firm seems on the up-and-up.

But suppose you don't know any agents at all? You may want to start your search for the perfect agent by examining the real estate firm for which he or she works. Large or small, the types of firms you are likely to encounter usually are in one of two business categories:

- *An independently owned company.* Usually going by names such as Joseph Smith Real Estate Agency, Inc., independents are likely to be home-grown and owned by either one entity (Joseph Smith) or Smith and a partner or two. Some homesellers prefer independent agencies because such companies can operate in ways that are tailored to the customers in their local markets, without kowtowing to a home office halfway across the country.

- *A franchise.* You've probably heard of several of the bigger franchises: Century 21® or ReMax, for example. Some buyers prefer franchises because the corporation often provides opportunities for continuing education to sales agents working for its brokers. Second, a far-flung corporation has branches virtually everywhere. Suppose you enlist a franchised broker to sell your house. You're moving because you have just been transferred to Hawaii. Chances are that this type of broker will be able to connect you with his or her associates in that state, making your relocation easier.

Different types of brokerage firms operate within these major categories. They include traditional, discount, and menu of services brokers. They differ primarily in how they charge you for services rendered.

Brokers and sales agents work in a fairly high-overhead business. They often spend big bucks on marketing via newspaper ads, TV shows and spots, radio commercials, billboards, direct mail—you name it. This helps attract new clients. Agency owners also have to foot the bill for the salaries of support staff, office upkeep, and so forth.

The gist of this is you can expect to hand over a healthy check to any broker once he or she sells your house. Brokers are no different, in this regard, than other professionals who render services, including doctors and lawyers.

Here's a list of the different types of brokerage firms and how they charge for their services.

- *Traditional brokerage firms.* These firms are paid a percentage of the sale price. What percentage? It really varies. Six percent isn't uncommon. Neither is 7 or 8 percent. Some may even charge 12 percent and up. Commissions are always negotiable.

- *Flat fee or discount brokers.* These brokers offer a flat fee for service, regardless of the sale price of your house. It's a "we'll-sell-your-house-for-five-grand" kind of game. When flat-fee brokers participate in a multiple listing service—cooperating with traditional brokers—they will likely negotiate two separate fees: a flat fee for themselves and a percentage fee for any cooperating broker.

- *A menu of services broker.* These firms offer a menu of services with separate prices for each. You choose, and pay for, only the services you want. These can include open houses and flyers distributed to cooperating agents; "feedback" calls to agents who have shown your house; and marketing support.

How You Pay

Most brokers in the United States operate on a traditional commission basis. Commission is the amount of money you pay to your broker for selling your house. As discussed above, the amount is a percentage of your house's actual sale price.

Once your house is sold, you make out a check to the broker. For the sake of argument, let's say that the check is 7 percent of the sale price. The broker, in turn, pays the sales agent a percentage of that 7 percent.

Suppose, though, an agent from another agency actually brings the buyers to the deal.

Then things get a little more complicated for the professionals involved, not for you. Instead of two people (your broker and agent) divvying up the 7 percent commission, you now have four—your broker, your agent, the agent who actually sold your house, and the agent's broker.

The good news is that even if 32 agents and brokers are somehow involved in the sale of your property, you are never responsible for more than the original, contracted for commission amount—in this case, 7 percent of the sales price.

These scenarios should also be taken into account before you decide on a discount broker. Here's why. Suppose the broker has agreed to sell your $200,000 house for a $5,000 flat fee. Few agents from outside the brokerage firm will bother to bring buyers through. Even if your broker splits the commission 50–50, most agents simply will not bother with a $200,000 sale that will only make $2,500 for the firm. (For one thing, the agent might only make a tad more than a grand off the sale.) This sale simply won't be worth the time and effort.

However, this shouldn't necessarily discourage you from employing a discount broker. Such an agency may write its contract so that it and its agents only demand $5,000 for the sale of your house but, if another agency sells the place, you agree to pay a commission to that firm in addition to the $5,000. Again, rates of commission can vary.

Make Sure You Respect the Broker

To get a feel for the company you're thinking of employing, call and ask to speak to the broker-owner or the sales manager. Tell them you're thinking of putting your house on the market and that you would like to stop by for a chat. Schedule an appointment and make sure you meet at the broker's place of business.

Having coffee with a broker or sales manager at a local cafe might seem more pleasant than trekking across town to the broker's office, but you need to spend time in the office to get a feel for how the organization is run.

When you're there, check out the following:

- The professionalism of the receptionist

- The level of business activity in the office. If you happen upon a bunch of real estate agents doing crosswords, painting their fingernails, or chatting

with their spouses on the phone, you might want to consider a more aggressive operation.

- The number of times the telephone rings. A dead phone isn't a great sign.

- The demeanor of the broker or manager. Does the broker seem to be a straight-shooter? Is he or she happy to take the time to speak with you?

Here's an example.

Martin McGuire, real estate sales manager, has hung a poster of a donkey on the wall behind his desk. The poster bears the legend, "We love to get kicked." On his desk sits a framed inspirational card. The sentiment reads, "When you're this low, the only place you can go is up." The office itself is organized in the "let stuff fall in piles all over the floor and I'll look for it later" method. Your empathies might go out to a disorganized but hard-working guy having trouble making a buck, but you probably don't want to list your house with the firm he represents.

Across town, Lara Kinley, owner of a small but well-respected firm, has hung on her office wall a framed and matted version of the company's logo: "We don't want to be the biggest, just the best." On her desk sits the company's powerful vision statement, a half-full inbox, and a brimming outbox. Several filing cabinets line her far wall.

The savvy homeseller would likely pick Kinley's firm over McGuire's. Visit the broker's office. It can tell you a lot about the overall operation.

Questions for Brokers

You can also ask the broker or manager some specific questions that will clue you in on how competent the firm is and how it conducts its business. Here are ten of those questions and some replies you should listen for.

1. *Is your firm independently owned or franchised? Why have you chosen to go solo or have you taken the franchise route?* The owner of a sound independent firm should reply, "We like being able to make decisions on our own, decisions that best support the buyers and sellers in our particular

market. We don't want to have to rely on administrative decisions made for an entire country." Or: "The money we save in franchise fees goes directly toward our marketing efforts. We position ourselves well in the community and we take great care in marketing individual houses to the selected group of house hunters most likely to buy." The representative of a franchised company might respond to your question with, "Not only are we able to pool resources and provide greater exposure of our clients' houses, we enjoy state-of-the-art training and ideas that give us a competitive edge."

2. *How long have your been in business?* In some markets, you'll find one or two extremely well-established agencies. Often these are family-owned independents, operating in some cases for more than a century. Because of their reputation and contacts, any other brokers operating in the area will likely look like pale upstarts in comparison. In other markets you'll find that franchised operations rule the roost, both in terms of corporate stability and visibility. Clearly, you don't have to go with the oldest company in your town. The age of an operation, however, can point to its stability and to its ability to sell houses in your market.

3. *How many listings are currently in your multiple listing service database? How many are comparable to ours?* This question will help you determine whether you operate in a buyer's or seller's market. If the broker answers, "Very few. This is an older area so it's rare to find a house that has four bedrooms like yours—most have only two or three. And the four-bedroom houses that do come on the market are usually snapped up by couples with growing families," you'll know that you're operating in a strong seller's market. If the broker answers "tons," understand that the market may have swayed to the buyer's advantage. If so, prepare for a long wait to sell and put the thought of trying to sell your house on your own out of your mind. Real estate agents are even more important in a buyer's market.

4. *What are the prices of the houses you market?* Just because the company has a substantial number of houses for sale doesn't mean it markets houses in

your price range. (Learn how to determine your price range in chapter 6.) The broker may even be unable or unwilling to market your house. Let's say you're selling a $50,000 starter home. A brokerage firm called Mansions R Us would likely politely refuse to take you on as a client. You'd have to find a different broker. Of course, the firm may simply not have any properties comparable to yours (similar in size, location, and amenities) at the moment because it's a really hot market and your type of house no sooner goes on the block than a sound offer rolls in. Lucky duck.

5. *What's your average list-to-sale ratio? What's the average list-to-sale ratio throughout the local multiple listing service?* A list-to-sale ratio is simply the difference between what you market your house for and the price a buyer actually pays for it. Your broker may tell you that his or her agents generally sell houses for 5 percent below list. Is this a good or a bad figure? It depends. If you learn that the average multiple listing service list-to-sale ratio in your area is 8 percent below the asking price, you should strongly consider going with the broker to whom you are now speaking. You would earn, on average, 3 percent more from the sale of your house. Think of it this way. You're listing your house for $100,000. If, on average, brokers in your area sell houses for 8 percent below list, you'd likely end up actually unloading your home for $92,000. If the broker that you're now meeting with says that his or her agents, on average, sell properties for 5 percent below list, you could expect to sell your house for $95,000 by going with that company.

6. *What's your average period from placing a house on the market to selling it?* You may like to get a broker known for a quick turn-around time. Ask this question of several different agencies.

7. *How many sales associates work for your company?* If a firm is only a two- or three-person operation, you may need to consider whether it is staffed at all times to handle phone inquiries and walk-ins from potential buyers.

8. *How many full-time sales associates work for you?* Only go with a full-time agent. As a very general rule of thumb, someone who makes a living sell-

ing real estate is more likely to keep abreast of financing deals, local market conditions, and marketing trends. If the majority of agents working for your broker only sell real estate part-time, you may want to consider another company. For the chunk of change you'll eventually hand the broker, you want full-time service.

9. *What compensation do you offer to other brokerage firms that assist in the sale of my house?* If your house is listed in a multiple listing database, chances are that sales agents other then your own will show the place. One of them may even sell it. That, of course, assumes that your broker offers reasonable commission compensation to cooperating sales agents. (See "How You Pay" on page 20.) With this question, you figure out how this broker slices the commission pie. If a broker offers a ridiculously low percentage to other real estate agencies, those agencies may be hesitant to bring people through your house. They're going to want to go where they can make the most money on comparable deals. And your property would lose some of the exposure it needs.

10. *Which of your agents do you think would be right for me?* During your conversation the broker will ask you about your goals for selling your house. If you have determined that this particular broker is one you might want to work with, take the time now to ask which of the firm's agents he or she thinks would best meet your needs. Remember, after narrowing your list of potential brokers you'll have to start building your list of potential agents.

Interviewing a series of brokers will take several hours' work on your part. But building a relationship with an agency that you trust is well worth the effort.

Finding an Agent

Because you will work primarily with a real estate agent, not a broker, your choice of an agent will prove to be even more important than your choice of a real estate firm. As noted above, you can meet with brokers first and ask them to recommend agents or you can search for a sales agent yourself. Here are some good sources:

- *Your friends.* If your friends Harry and Sally couldn't be more pleased with the professionalism of real estate agent Jean Jones, you might want to consider giving Jean a call. Remember, though: Make sure that friends doing the recommending understand that you want to sell your house for the best price possible in your market. You don't want to hire an agent if your best friend recommends him solely because "He's my brother's cousin, and I want to toss him a break."

- *People you know.* You're more likely to trust, and work well with, agents you're acquainted with. These might be neighbors, friends, members of your church, members of local civic organization to which you belong, or even a relative.

- *Agents you've met.* If you're selling, you're moving. Maybe you've already begun to check out the local real estate market. If you've met an agent you like through an open house or a private showing, by all means ask for his or her card. This person may prove to be the right agent to market your house. If you're house hunting, pay special attention to agents who respond to your questions, provide you with material on the house you're touring, offer you some type of brochure, and disclose any flaws in the house you're touring. These are all signs of a competent professional.

- *Agents who advertise.* Watch real estate agents' advertisements on television, listen to them on the radio, and read them in the newspapers. How many houses are they listing? How do those houses compare with yours? If an agent seems extraordinarily busy, there's usually a reason. It's because that agent is good.

Questions for Agents

Once you have compiled a list of a half-dozen or so prospective agents, concentrating on full-time salespeople only, invite each to your house for separate question-and-answer sessions. If you have selected an agent before you have chosen a broker, you may want to first ask several of the questions listed under "Make Sure You

Respect the Broker" on page 21. However, if you are interviewing agents recommended to you by a broker, you can start right in on the specifics with the following seven questions:

1. *How many years have you been in the business?* An agent who has been hustling for a long time should have the recommendations and reputation to prove it. A green agent, meanwhile, may be motivated, hungry, and brimming with new ideas. This is a decision only you can make. What you don't want is someone who has been merely coasting for 20 years.

2. *What professional designations do you hold?* Here are some things you probably don't care about. The Graduate Realtor Institute of the National Association of Realtors requires students to take 90 hours of classroom work in fields ranging from time management to marketing. To be deemed a Certified Residential Specialist, agents take additional classes and must have a fairly strong track record. Boring. Dull as dust. But any real estate agent who comes to you with at least some accreditation beyond a license demonstrates a true career interest and time (and sometimes money) honing skills. Such an agent is a pro, and you want to go with a pro.

3. *How many sellers and buyers do you currently represent?* You want an agent who is busy, but not sooooooooo busy that he or she gives your house a low priority. Agents in some metropolitan areas may work well with as many as ten buyers and sellers at once. In other areas, agents may only be comfortable working with five people at a time. Find out the norm for your area by looking around.

4. *How many properties have you sold in the last year? What type of properties were they?* Compare this agent's sales record with those of other salespeople you're interviewing. Ask how long, on average, it took to close these deals and what type of units were sold. An agent who seems to specialize in condos may not be the best choice to market your four-bedroom farmhouse. An agent who specializes in houses in the $500,000-and-up range may give your modest, $65,000 cottage very low priority.

5. *Can you provide me a list of references?* You should contact customers this agent has served over the last several years to see if they were satisfied with the work performed on their behalf. See the "Checking References" sidebar on page 29 for details.

6. *Do you work on your own or are you part of a real estate team?* Often, two agents will join forces and operate as a real estate team. This can be a great deal for the seller because you essentially get two professionals for the price of one. If your potential agent, however, works as part of a team, make sure you meet the other member or members. You want to feel comfortable with everyone involved in the process.

7. *Is there anything else you'd like to tell me about yourself, your company, or your career?* This is a catchall question and an honest agent may reveal some interesting facts—notably, plans for a job change or agency plans to merge with a competitor.

Deciding on the Big Three

Through one-on-one interviews, narrow your agent field to three contenders. Then ask each of them to prepare a more formal presentation for you.

This presentation should include a comparable marketing analysis (CMA). The analysis lists the selling prices of houses similar to yours and is used as a guide for you and your agent to determine how to price your place. The presentation should also include an overall marketing plan for the house.

The agent's demeanor, the thought behind this presentation, and your overall compatibility should help you determine which salesperson is right for you.

The Listing

A listing is nothing more than a contract—called a *listing agreement*—giving a broker the right to act as your representative in the sale of a property.

Checking References

As a general rule, you'll want to contact at least six references, ideally the agent's clients, who are provided to you by your agent. Try to speak with people who have sold properties comparable to the one you're placing on the market. Here are some questions you should ask.

- Did the agent make few promises but keep the ones made? You don't want an agent who promises you the earth and delivers a handful of dust.

- Did you have regular contact with the agent—not an assistant or a secretary—during the selling process? You're going to end up paying your agent a fair amount of cash. Your agent owes you accessibility.

- Did the agent keep you informed? You'll need to know if your agent contacts customers regularly, relating buyer feedback, and keeping them apprised of how negotiations are progressing.

- How long did it take the agent to sell your house?

And of course, you'll want to ask the ultimate, end-all question: Would you use this agent again?

The type of listing you decide on can help determine how the house is marketed and who gets to show it. Remember, you want your house to receive the largest exposure possible. Here are the most common types of listings.

The Open Listing

This agreement allows your real estate agency to sell your house and collect a specified commission. Through this contract, you can list your house with as many brokers as you like. If you end up selling the house yourself, you owe nothing to any of the firms involved.

Sounds like a nifty deal, doesn't it? You can have 20 firms, all working busily to sell your house. But there's a catch.

If you place your house with several real estate firms, they may each independently decide that the competition among salespeople seeking to unload this property is simply too stiff. They may decide to spend little or no time marketing your house or bringing buyers through it. So instead of a bunch of people working for you full time, you may end up with a bunch of people working for you no time.

The Exclusive Listing

You promise to list your house with one brokerage firm only and that company promises to do everything it can to sell the property. This usually includes placing it in a multiple listing service database to elicit the assistance of other agents who may know of buyers interested in the property. (Most multiple listing service's won't take anything but exclusive right to sell contracts.)

Again, this agreement allows you to sell the house yourself, and you are under no obligation to pay anyone a commission if you do so.

The Exclusive Right to Sell

This contract allows you to list your house with only one brokerage firm and that firm receives its commission even if you sell the house on your own. The firm agrees to do everything it can to sell the property. Again, this usually includes marketing, inclusion in a multiple listing service database, and cooperation with other real estate agents.

The exclusive right to sell contract is often a homeowner's best bet because agents tend to work hardest under this type of agreement.

The Listing Agreement Form

If you're like most sellers, you'll probably end up deciding on an exclusive agency or exclusive right to sell listing. The following information will be included on the listing contract:

- Type of listing

- Names of the parties involved

- List price

- Length of the agreement

- Commission, written as a percentage of the eventual sale, or as a flat fee, or as the total cost of individual services

- Broker protection clause (provides for the broker to collect a commission if he or she has procured a buyer before the listing agreement's expiration date but was unable to close the transaction until afterward)

- List of personal property (drapes, appliances, etc.) that you plan to sell with the house

- Permission for the broker to market the house (including placing a For Sale sign on the front lawn, showing the house during reasonable hours by appointment, and placing a lockbox on the front door for access by cooperating agents)

- Permission to place the house on a multiple listing service

- Equal Opportunity statement (noting that no one can be denied access to the house because of race, color, religion, sex, disability, and so forth)

- Fact sheet on the property (listing the house's amenities and specifics such as size, taxes, and school district)

- Signatures of all parties

Bottom-Line Thinking

By now, you should have a clue about:

- How the brokerage business works, including brokers' responsibilities to their clients

- How the sales agent fits into the picture

- How the broker gets paid

- Choosing a brokerage firm and an agent

- What's in a listing agreement

GOING Solo

Before deciding whether to take the "by owner" route, consider whether you have the time, energy, and knowledge to pull off a sale. And remember, while selling a house yourself is cheaper than employing a real estate agent, you will have to hire and pay for experts—from lawyers to home inspectors—to help. You'll also probably spend a few bucks on marketing efforts.

The chapter will examine the advantages and disadvantages of the for sale by owner (FSBO) world and help you decide whether it's the one for you. You'll learn about:

- The advantages and disadvantages of selling by owner

- Creating a "dream team" of experts for guidance

- Marketing your house

- Qualifying potential buyers

- Showing your house

Do-It-Yourself

If you have read this far and decided to sell your house yourself, you are no longer a person. You are a FSBO (pronounced fizz-bow). Both you and your property will be referred to by this acronym, especially by the real estate agents who'll practically go into conniptions trying to explain how your house would sell much more quickly, and at a better price, if only you employed their services.

There are a number of reasons to drive a for sale by owner sign into your front yard. Let's take a look at a few of them.

Saving on the commission. Most brokers charge the seller a commission for closing on a house. This is usually somewhere between 6 and 8 percent of the sale price. Though most good agents really do earn their commission, it's still a large chunk of change. You may need that money for other purposes.

Take the Williamsons as an example. They chose to sell their $185,000 house on their own when they learned that the brokerage fee—based on 7 percent of the sale price— would total $12,950. Because the Williamsons only had a little more than $32,000 equity in their house, they realized that paying an agent to sell the house would leave them with too little cash to make a substantial down payment on a new place.

Lack of trust. Unfortunately, the real estate field, as all professional fields, has a few bum members. People often decide to sell their houses themselves after suffering through bad experiences with real estate agents.

The Nelsons are an example. Twice before they'd sold their houses, each time hiring salespeople who offered glowing presentations and promises to sell the house at a very good price—a price that later proved inflated. Once hired, both agents provided the Nelsons with very minimal marketing support. The houses sold only after long stints on the market, and then at prices far lower than the Nelsons had been led to expect. Now that a job transfer requires the couple to move again, they have decided to sell their house by themselves.

A buyer in your pocket. Perhaps you know someone who once said to you "I love your house. If you ever decide to sell, please call me first." So you call. It turns out that this person still wants to buy and is offering a handsome price. There's really no need for you to bring a real estate agent or broker into this type of situation.

The seller's market. A seller's market occurs when more buyers are looking for houses than there are properties for sale. This is a sound scenario in which to try to sell your house yourself.

Challenge. If you love a challenge, like to take control of any situation, and want to see what you can do with a piece of real estate—go for it!

Or maybe not.

As you've undoubtedly guessed by now, the FSBO world offers as many pitfalls as it does peaks. The downside is that your inexperience may lead you to sell for a lot less than your house is worth and to take too long finding a buyer.

Let's look at some of the problems you may face.

Pricing the house. Of course you want a sound price for your palace. But what, exactly, is that price? Clearly, you probably don't want buyers to lick their lips thinking, "This is the steal of the century. Cheap at quadruple the price." Conversely, you don't want to price yourself out of the market.

Showing the house. You probably try to make your house look its best whenever you have company, but preparing it for a prospective buyer is another story. You may need to renovate or repair, including, perhaps, new paint or new landscaping. You may not know how to spot the areas that need sprucing up but a real estate agent will.

You also have to learn the techniques and deal with the inconvenience of showing the house to prospective buyers. In their eagerness to sell, homeowners make big mistakes showing a property, mainly out of inexperience in "reading" the customer.

Take the Royersons, for example. Tom and Angie assumed that everyone wants a big house, so, when showing their property, Angie waxed poetic about the spaciousness of the house, the huge primary rooms, the large entry foyer, the bigger-than-average bedrooms. The potential buyers left feeling that the house was too big when, really, it was the perfect size for their needs.

Marketing the property. Marketing your house isn't as easy as taking out a full-page spread in your local newspaper, one announcing in huge type: BEAUTIFUL HOME FOR SALE! A REAL BARGAIN!

You need to concentrate your marketing efforts on those consumers most likely to buy in your price range. You also have to figure out how to differentiate your house from all the comparable properties for sale in the area—including those that are getting lots of attention through a multiple listing service.

It's a tricky marketing goal: setting your house apart and dragging the right sorts of consumers in for a look-see.

Qualifying the buyer. You need to make sure that any potential buyer boasts the financial wherewithal to actually get a mortgage to purchase your house. Before deciding whether to sell by owner, consider whether you feel comfortable asking potential buyers how much they earn, how much of their savings they will invest, and so forth.

Negotiating. Many homesellers dread negotiation—and everything that happens between buyers making a first offer and closing on the deal. Other than when hosting a garage sale, you may have never before faced anyone haggling over price. And face it, you're going to be far more willing to drop a few bucks off the price of your old maternity clothing than to drop a few grand off the price of your house.

But because it is the rare buyer who will match your list price right out of the box, you need to understand the minimum price you can financially walk away with and what you are willing to compromise in order to meet that goal.

If That Is the Law

You'll almost certainly have to hire a lawyer to help you through the legalities of selling your house. You don't want to lose a sale, for example, because you didn't know that you were required to reveal any structural defects in the house. Worse, you don't want to complete the sale, have the buyer move in and find out that the heating system is being held together with some spit and rubber bands, and then sue you for not divulging this problem.

Inconvenience. Potential buyers don't house hunt on your schedule. They may only be able to see the place at 2:30 on a Wednesday afternoon. Suppose you work outside the home. Are you in a position to leave your job at a moment's notice to run home for a showing?

If your job is particularly high pressure, you also need to consider whether you'll have the time to return buyer phone calls promptly and put together a marketing plan for your house.

Money. A final caveat: Even people who choose to sell their houses sans brokers don't truly work on their own. They end up hiring lawyers, escrow officers, tax consultants, home inspectors, and their ilk. More than one homeseller, sitting back to take stock after the deal closed, has determined that the expenses of hiring these professionals, coupled with his or her own hard work, were greater than the cost of selling the house through an agent.

Even Do-It-Yourselfers Need Some Outside Help

John Donne wrote that "no man is an island." Similarly, no FSBO ever sold a house entirely on his own. Successful homesellers surround themselves with a veritable dream team of real estate experts. Unless your sale should prove to be exceptionally complicated, the fees these professionals charge are usually minimal but their advice is invaluable. Here are the folks you have to meet.

Someone's Knocking at the Door, Somebody's Ringing the Bell

Ah, yes. You put up your FSBO sign yesterday, and today the telephone rings. Your heart skips a beat. Your first prospective buyer. Then this is what you hear.

"Hi. This is Susan Montgomery calling form Sell-A-Lot Real Estate. I was wondering if you know that many people are able to get higher prices for their houses, and sell them more quickly, working with a real estate agent than on their own?"

Grrrrrrr.

This type of call may anger you. You've announced to the world your decision to sell your house yourself. Why, then, do real estate agents call you?

They're always on the prowl for new listings, and they know you want to sell the place.

A professional yard sign should do much to cut back on the number of calls you receive from agents. The fact that you're spending a few bucks to have it done professionally indicates that you're a serious FSBO. If agents do call, of course, you can politely say "No thank you" and hang up. If you are contacted by an agent you really like, you may want to ask for some information about that agent and his or her company. You can keep that info on file, just in case selling your house by owner proves too much of a hassle.

Real Estate Appraiser

A reputable real estate appraiser can help you decide how to price your house at market value. You use the appraisal documentation when showing the house to potential buyers or during negotiations. It's hard for the average consumer to argue with the opinion of a trained professional.

Home Inspector

Because nondisclosure of defects in your house can lead to lost sales and lawsuits, home inspections are essential. If an inspector finds a problem, you can fix it before officially putting the house on the market, making for a smoother eventual sale. And, of course, if you have already paid for a home inspection, your buyer won't have to. Buyers are probably looking to save a few bucks wherever they can, so a previously completed inspection can prove to be a draw.

A home inspection should cover such structural items as foundations, cement slabs, crawl spaces, roofing, walls, floors, ceilings, windows, and doors. An inspector will determine whether they are strong enough to support the weight of the house.

The inspector will also evaluate all exposed water and waste pipes, faucets, water heaters, drainage systems, heating and cooling systems, and will check for environmental hazards such as radon.

Don't hire an inspector who also performs repair work. You don't want the inspector stumbling upon problems merely to make work—and money.

Tax Adviser

Strictly speaking, you don't absolutely need a tax adviser when selling your house. But these professionals can assist you in structuring your sale to maximize your tax savings. Make sure you find someone who has experience in real estate tax issues. Ask your real estate agent or accountant for a referral.

Escrow Officer

An escrow officer is a disinterested third party in a real estate transaction. This person holds, in an escrow account, money that is likely to change hands as long as certain conditions are met. Here's an example.

A buyer makes a first offer on your property and is willing to put up $2,000 in earnest money. As the term implies, this cash shows that the buyer is serious about purchasing the house. But a savvy consumer will make the offer contingent on your house passing inspection.

Under these circumstances, do you think the buyer is just going to write you a check for two grand? Of course not. The house might flunk inspection, and a crotchety seller might be disinclined to return this poor buyer's money.

The $2,000 goes into an escrow account, to be released to you if the house passes inspection, and to be released back to the would-be buyer if it fails and other accommodations aren't made.

Your escrow or closing officer can be a lawyer, banker, or representative of the firm that issues title insurance. In many areas, it may be the listing broker. And although you likely won't need to actually employ an escrow officer until you receive your first offer, it's a good idea to have one or two standing by from the time you place your house on the market. You never know when a buyer will show up, and you don't want to stall the sale by searching around for an escrow officer after you've gotten a bite.

Consulting Real Estate Agent

Need a hand wading through the FSBO process? You might want to hire a real estate agent—not to *actually* sell your house but to offer advice on how you can *best* sell your house. The agent might charge an hourly rate or, if you're very lucky, provide this service for free in hopes of getting future business. Ask your consulting real estate agent questions you have regarding the showing and marketing of your house, negotiations, and closing.

Remember that the agent can only provide professional advice and cannot give you any legal advice—you need a lawyer for that.

Real Estate Lawyer

If you're a FSBO, you'll need one. The lawyer's role on your dream team is discussed extensively in chapter 4.

Nice Place
Ya' Got, Here

Use the following worksheet to identify the amenities in your house.

1. What first attracted us to our house before buying was:_____

2. Was this initial attraction a factor in our decision to buy?

_____

Why or why not?_____

3. Other amenities that lured us into buying the house were:

_____

4. Since we've moved in, we've learned to appreciate these things about our house:

_____

To Market, To Market

After assembling your dream team, you need to determine how to advertise and otherwise market your house to reach the buyer you want. Remember, exposure is the key.

Before considering target markets and marketing strategies, think back a bit. When you bought the house, what feature most appealed to you? It might have been the location, the wooded backyard, the gourmet kitchen, the fireplace in the master bedroom, or a host of other amenities.

Whatever attracted you to the property will likely draw a new buyer as well. Sit down and list your house's features, then think about who would likely appreciate them.

For example, a cozy, one-story ranch may be perfect for a retired couple that no longer likes to use the stairs. Proximity to the best elementary school in the county will draw families with young children. The bachelor with two golden retrievers might drool over your large, fenced-in backyard. These people become the "target" audience for your marketing plan. (Keep in mind, though, that fair housing laws prohibit explicit advertising for retirees or bachelors or families with no children.)

How to begin marketing? Think about the yard sign.

The Professional Yard Sign

Forgo the $5 orange-and-black For Sale signs that you can pick up at any Megamart. Most of your calls will result from a yard sign, so you want to invest in one with a little bit of style.

Have one professionally made to look like those used by real estate agents. It should be about 20 inches by 30 inches; colorful, but not garish.

Here's the information you should include on the sign.

- *The words* For Sale By Owner. Lots of people want to avoid real estate agents and brokers, so your property's FSBO status is a draw. Make sure these words are written in letters large enough to attract passing motorists.

How Do You Find
These People?

We've talked about the necessity of assembling a FSBO dream team. But you may not know how to find the right professionals to help you.

First, try to get recommendations from friends, relatives, and, even—when hiring home inspectors or appraisers—local lending institutions.

If you're having a hard time, simply turn to the yellow pages of your local phone book. This is what you should look for:

- *Home inspectors.* Professionals who advertise with the letters ASHI after their names are members of the American Society of Home Inspectors. They must have a certain level of experience and education to join. Note: In some places, custom dictates that the seller pays for a home inspection. In others, the buyer is expected to foot the bill.

- *Appraisers.* Initials such as MAI, SRA, or SREA appearing behind the contact's name indicate that the appraiser belongs to one of several professional associations, has taken continuing education courses, and has agreed to uphold a code of ethics.

- *Tax adviser.* Look for a CPA (Certified Public Accountant) with real estate experience.

- *One feature of your house.* This feature should attract attention from members of your target market. Use phrases such as "3 Bedroom/2 Bath" or "Spacious Family Room." You don't want your sign to look cluttered but what if you want to emphasize more than one feature? Easy. Have your sign built with a removable bar across its stake. The feature touted should appear only on that information bar. You can remove the bar periodically and replace it with another that highlights a different feature.

- *The words* By Appointment Only. You don't want to show your house to everyone who may just be looking around during a Sunday drive. You want to get any potential buyer on the telephone first to ensure a legitimate interest in the house and the means to secure a mortgage.

- *Your telephone number.* Make sure the numerals are large enough to be read from the street by a motorist driving at about 30 miles per hour. And make sure there is always someone or something (i.e., an answering machine) on call for this number.

- *An information box.* Drive this box into your front lawn next to the yard sign. It should contain fliers detailing all things wonderful about your house and listing the nitty-gritty: price, square feet, taxes, school district, and so forth. Paint, or have painted, the phrase "Free! Take One" on the side. You can easily create these fliers yourself, either on a home computer or in a public office center such as Kinko's. Make sure to include an attractive picture of your house.

Your local zoning board may regulate signs in residential neighborhoods. Check to see what, if any, restrictions it will place on your placard. If your zoning board allows, consider having your message printed on both sides of your sign, and place the sign perpendicular to your house so that motorists heading in both directions can read it. If you live on a corner, consider investing in two sides to capture the attention of traffic traveling on either street.

Publicity

Clearly, you cannot just stick up a yard sign and think, "Great! My marketing efforts are now complete." You need to start garnering some real publicity for your product—your house.

There are two kinds of publicity: the free kind, and the kind you pay for. Cash-only advertising venues may better target the audience you hope to reach. But free publicity never hurt anyone, and has helped find buyers for more than a few FSBOs.

Free Stuff

Remember those flyers we talked about above? Print out a bunch, and place them wherever a buyer is likely to look. These include:

- College bulletin boards, especially those near adult/continuing education offices or classrooms.

- Human resources or housing departments of large corporations, hospitals, military installations, and the like.

- Bulletin boards in fitness centers, shopping centers, grocery stores, cleaners, laundries, libraries, civic centers, community centers, and anywhere else you can think of.

- In the hands of friends. Send one or two of your flyers to everyone in your address book. Hand them to everyone you see regularly, including your coworkers, friends, neighbors, relatives, church members, bowling league colleagues, and so on. If none of these people are interested in buying a new house, ask them to keep the flyers around in case they run into anyone who is.

Also remember to give a flyer to anyone who comes to an open house (discussed later in this chapter). Potential buyers view a lot of properties, and having a flyer in hand will help refresh their memories on all things wonderful in your house.

"STONEY CREEK"
22 WILD HORSE ROAD
PLEASANT VALLEY
$420,000

WHERE MOTHER NATURE IS THE DEVELOPER

Romantic . . . Classic . . . Comfortable. What better way to describe this gorgeous Country French 1 1/2 Story Home in one of the Most Sought After areas . . . Stoney Creek. The unique floor plan allows a gorgeous view from every room, of deer, wildlife, Stoney Bluff and Creek.

Upon entering, you will experience the many distinguished features welcoming you HOME! The impressive wood flooring follows through the Hearth Room, Kitchen, Powder Room, and Foyer. In the stunning Great Room, you will be drawn to the enticing Fireplace flanked by a Custom Entertainment Center and Bookcases. The wall of circle-top windows frames this beautiful picture. The Study is enveloped with richly stained wood and complimented by Custom Bookcases and Window Seats. The legendary beauty continues in the Kitchen and Hearth Rooms. Eggshell Legacy Cabinets, complimented with a Pine Designer Island, assures lasting beauty in the efficient Kitchen, while the Hearth Room, accented with a Stone Fireplace, opens onto an expansive deck.

The center of serenity . . . the Master Suite . . . is secluded on the main level, offering the ultimate in convenience and privacy, with a rear deck. The upper level offers two Bedrooms sharing a Jack & Jill Bath, and a third Bedroom or Guest Bedroom with a Private Bath.

The walk-out Lower Level enables future expansion.

For Your Private Showing, Please Call . . .
555-1426

Information deemed reliable but not guaranteed.

The House Book

Used as a marketing tool while showing a house to buyers, a house book is a book about, well, your house. On the first page, it should have color photographs of your home, the address, and a complete legal description. Other pages should include a copy of your flyer; before-and-after pictures of any remodeling projects you may have undertaken; tax information; the dimensions of the lot; and photocopies of utility bills incurred during different times of the year. Also include the Seller Disclosure of Property Condition Form and the Lead-Based Paint Disclosure Form. (See chapter 4 for details.) Remember, this book stays in your house and is used solely for perusal by those touring the property.

Stuff You Pay For

You'd make out like a bandit if all advertising was as easy and cheap as the cost of printing up some flyers and tacking them to various bulletin boards. Of course, it just doesn't work that way. While free advertising certainly lures buyers on occasion, your chances of reaching the family that will absolutely fall in love with your house escalates when you invest a few bucks in some common advertising venues. These include classified advertising, the Internet, and radio.

Classified advertising. Place a for sale advertisement in whichever area newspaper boasts the greatest number of housing ads. And place the ad on the day the newspaper carries the largest for sale ad volume—usually a Sunday.

Study these advertisements several weeks in advance of placing your own ad. Determine which ads grab your attention, and mimic them.

Here are some guidelines:

- *Title.* Each ad should have a title or heading that grabs the attention of potential buyers. The title, usually typed in bold, can read: "By Owner" or "A Real Deal," for example. Then note the price. This allows buyers to determine, off the bat, whether it's a property they can afford. You don't want to waste time fielding offers from people who can't possibly secure financing for your house.

- *Location.* Discuss the location, noting the subdivision or area of town in which your house sits. Do not, however, give your exact address. Remember, you don't want drop-ins, and you'll certainly get them if you provide your address.

- *Size.* Note the house's size, including square feet and the number of bedrooms and bathrooms. Also mention any outstanding feature—a formal garden, a workshop/garage, and so forth.

- *Action statement.* Conclude with a call to action or a phrase such as "Call now. This one won't last long" or "Don't delay. You may lose your chance to buy this one-of-a kind jewel." Include a telephone number. Again, make sure either a person or a machine is available to answer this phone at all times.

Internet. Consider listing your house on any of the FSBO sites now operating on the Internet. These ads can help you lure both local customers and people who may be relocating to your town from other parts of the country. Prices for these listings vary, so shop around before deciding. Try For Sale By Owner Network (http://www.f-s-b-o.com/) or By Owner Online (http://www.by-owner-ol.com/) for starters.

Television. Television spots, 30 seconds or a minute, can prove quite expensive if you're buying time on an early morning show or during the nightly news. The advent of public access channels, however, has afforded you with a reasonably priced TV advertising venue. You pay a nominal fee and prepare your own script or video. Make the script or video as professional as possible. Warning: It's very easy to make an impossibly cheesy homemade commercial. You want to make a good impression on prospective buyers, not make them laugh. Do the television thing carefully and professionally, or not at all.

Radio. You may find it worth your time (and ultimately, your cash) to contact several local stations, get the demographics of their audience, and their peak air times (usually drive time—when people are heading to or from work). You may choose to air a few short, strategic commercials to a specific target audience.

Showing the House

Don't be surprised if all your advertising efforts actually lure in some potential buyers. That was, after all, the point. Now you're going to have to learn how to show your house, both through public open houses and individual tours.

First, talk to potential buyers on the phone. Try to determine whether they have the cash to buy your home, and whether it's the type of property they want. Otherwise, all your work in showing the house will go for naught.

Here are some questions to ask callers:

- *What attracted you to my advertisement or sign?* You want to know what features hit buyers' hot buttons so that you can emphasize those amenities when it comes time to show them your house.

- *What other features are you looking for in a house?* Learn as much as possible about what the caller wants in a house so that you can again emphasize the features that match those desires.

- *Do you currently own or rent?* If buyers are already homeowners, they'll probably make purchase of your house contingent on selling theirs. This can potentially delay a sale. If the caller currently rents, ask when the lease expires. If the caller is locked into a lease for another six months, that can also delay your sale.

- *How long have you been looking for a home? How many homes have you seen?* Potential buyers look at a bunch of houses, typically buying between the eighth and fifteenth home they view. If your buyer started looking three days ago, it's probably too early to start packing your bags.

- *Have you seen any houses that you really liked?* If the buyers say yes, ask why they didn't buy. Maybe they couldn't sell their house in time and still haven't gotten an offer. Maybe they couldn't get financing. Maybe they couldn't escape their lease. Any of these issues could potentially delay or prevent them from buying your house. If the buyers have not yet seen a

home they really liked, you may wonder why. Maybe they have only looked at two houses so far. Or maybe they need a specific feature—for example, a five-acre lot for their palomino. If you don't have a five-acre lot, you probably shouldn't waste your time showing your house to these prospective buyers.

- *Are you looking on your own or with a real estate agent?* If the buyer is working with an agent, ask if you would need to pay some type of brokerage fee. Before granting a showing, discuss how much the fee would total, get it in writing, and decide whether it's an acceptable amount. Federal Trade Commission restrictions bar the establishment of fees, so no hard and fast rules exist for determining what this fee should be. The seller in a FSBO situation might pay the "selling portion" of the agent's commission, which might be as much as 3 to 4 percent (half of the agent's total 6 to 8 percent commission). These percentages are for example only. Remember, it's worth spending a few bucks if this caller ends up being your buyer.

- *Will anyone assist you in making a decision to purchase?* If mom and dad are footing part of the down payment, chances are mom and dad will want to see the house. Make sure that you arrange a showing time convenient for all persons involved in the sale.

- *Are you preapproved for a loan in this price range?* If the buyers have been preapproved, invite them over. If not, you have a whole slew of other questions to ask. Remember, you don't want to waste your time showing your place to people who can't get financing. Let them know you're asking to be sure you're not wasting their time. Here are some of the questions you should ask buyers who have *not* been preapproved for your price range: Where do you work? How long have you worked there? What is your position? Are you a one-income or a two-income household? What is your combined annual income? For what major debts are you responsible? Don't bother to show your house to callers who are unwilling to answer these questions or who do not seem to meet the earning power required to buy your house.

- *If you really like my house, how soon would you be prepared to close?* This question helps you determine whether your have serious or motivated buyers.

Finally, how do you know whether the buyer makes enough to buy your house? Generally, a buyer should spend only between 25 percent and 29 percent of gross monthly income for financial upkeep of a residence. This includes principal, interest, taxes, and insurance payments. Thirty-three percent to 41 percent of gross monthly income can go for the above plus outstanding monthly installment debts. Check with your local lenders for current financing programs and qualification requirements to best assess the information that you are receiving from the potential buyer.

If the buyer doesn't qualify, don't bother showing.

They're Here!

Once you've determined that the caller is a serious buyer, one capable of securing financing for your house, invite 'em over and show off the place. You'll find a lot of information on this subject in chapter 7. For now though, and before the prospect shows up, you have to get your house in order. This is what you do.

- Stand across the street and look at your house. Determine whether it looks clean, tidy, and inviting. If the lawn needs to be mowed or the garden weeded, do it. If the place needs to be painted, paint it.

- Clean! No kidding. Even the places you don't think any buyer would look—like the very, very back of your kitchen cupboards. Put your closets in order. A messy closet looks smaller. Conversely, nobody has ever refused a house because it has too much storage space.

- Open the drapes. Turn on the lights. Use your imagination so that all light sources combine to create a pleasant atmosphere. Stick some bread or cookies in the oven to give your house a nice, warm smell.

- Have a guest book available and ask everyone touring your house to sign. It allows you to follow up with potential buyers.

- Hide the good stuff. You never truly know who's touring your house. Stick the good jewelry someplace out of the way—and not your top dresser drawer. That's the first place any crook will look. Also hide small but valuable antiques, figurines, and the like. This is especially important during open houses, when you may get backed up and people are looking through your house alone.

That's your prep work; work discussed in much greater detail in chapter 6. Once the buyers show up, you should do the following things:

- Start with a tour of the grounds. It will whet your prospective buyer's appetite for the interior of your house.

- Plan out the rest of the route through your house. Make sure to end up someplace comfortable where you can chat a bit. Not the laundry room. And not someplace too comfortable, either—say the master bedroom. The kitchen, den, living or dining room is a great place to wind down.

- Don't walk into the kitchen and announce, "Here's the kitchen." The prospect will probably think, "No kidding, Sherlock." Instead, enter each room talking about its features. "What I've always loved about this kitchen," the savvy homeseller might say, "is the view from the window over the sink. Take a look. See that maple? It's always beautiful but during the fall the colors are so vibrant that it practically looks on fire. While you're here, would you like a glass of water? We have a purification system here and I think you can really taste the difference."

- Make sure the buyers sign your guest book and spend some time with your house book. Be certain that they see any necessary disclosures. Ascertain that you have answered all the buyers' questions. Ask the buyers how your house compares with other houses in this price range that they have toured. Ask them to be candid because it will help you to determine what you need to do to compete with the other properties that are being shown.

- Ask the buyers what it would take for them to prepare an offer on your house today. Listen very carefully. You'll find out how far apart you are on priorities. That's where negotiations begin. Strategies are discussed in chapter 8.

The Public Open House

The public open house is a common way to expose your house to potential buyers who prefer a casual tour to a scheduled, private showing.

Unfortunately, the laid-back nature of these events entices a fair number of "just-looking-arounders." Open houses simply are not nearly as effective as individual home showings are.

Still, you may decide to host an open house if several other such events are being held in your neighborhood. If you can coordinate your open house for the same day that Susie and Mark and Joanne and Rob are having theirs, their prospects will naturally stop at your place, too. You can also use the advertising techniques discussed above to draw buyers.

In addition to the prep work and touring techniques discussed for private showings, you should also:

- Have professionally lettered cards placed throughout your house to point out advantages that the buyer may otherwise miss. Examples might be, next to the furnace: New Furnace in 1999. In the kitchen: Turnstile for Easy-to-Reach Storage.

- Stay at the front door, welcome buyers when they enter, ask them to sign your guest book, and provide them with the flyer of your house. Invite them to tour on their own and to take their time with your house book. And offer to answer any questions on their way out.

Remember, when hosting an open house you need to keep your guests safe. Draw attention to any area that could prove hazardous by using large printed cards, caution signs, or bright yellow tape. If your prospect falls and breaks a hip on uneven steps, you've not only lost a sale, you may have "won" a lawsuit.

Succeeding as a FSBO

Now you know that selling your house is no easy feat. The entire task is in your hands—from assembling the dream team to marketing the property; from determining the price to closing the deal. It's a lot of work, and a lot of headaches. However, if you have the determination and the time, give it a try. Once the house sells you'll bask in the glow of a job well done, and the knowledge that you've saved a ton o' bucks by sidestepping commission fees.

Bottom-Line Thinking

By now, you should have a clue about:

- The advantages and disadvantages of selling on your own

- How to succeed as a FSBO by creating a dream team of experts to assist in the entire selling process

- Marketing your house

- Showing your house

- Qualifying the buyer

LAW and ORDER

CHAPTER FOUR

Let's talk about real estate law. Eyes glazing over yet? Relax. Take a chill pill. You really do need to know about this stuff.

Real estate law may never become your favorite subject but a sound layperson's knowledge of the rules governing home sales in your area will protect you from potential lawsuits. In this chapter, you'll get a clue about:

- Locating a reputable law firm

- Selecting and interviewing a lawyer

- Your legal rights

- Your legal obligations

- Fair housing requirements and how they affect you

- Disclosure forms

Finding a Lawyer

Having a lawyer on your side will help protect your interests during the course of the sale. If problems arise, you have someone to call. And even if no problems arise, sometimes just having a pro on your side will make you feel more comfortable with the whole process.

You need to find a lawyer who specializes in residential real estate transactions. You may already know one—like the lawyer who assisted you in buying your current property. If you liked him, hire him for the sale. If, however, you sought no legal help when you bought, you'll now need to embark on a search for a lawyer.

Your agent or the agent's broker can provide you with a list of several respected real estate lawyers working in your area. If you're selling FSBO, ask your friends, neighbors, relatives, or people you know through community organizations to recommend a real estate lawyer they trust.

You can also seek recommendations from:

- *Real estate agents you know.* In addition to your own agent, chances are your social/community circle includes at least a few members of the field. Ask them to recommend some property lawyers to you.

- *Mortgage lenders.* Call a few institutions and ask them for the names of real estate lawyers.

- *Appraisers, inspectors, and so forth.* Whether you're working FSBO or with a real estate agent, you're likely getting ready to hire appraisers, inspectors, and other professionals. Don't hesitate to ask these pros which real estate lawyers they respect.

Interviewing and Selecting the Right Lawyer

Compile a list of at least three highly recommended real estate lawyers. Call each of them at their office. Note that you are considering retaining this lawyer for a property transaction. Ask about a free initial consultation. If one is offered, terrific. Make an appointment. If all three lawyers offer this free service, meet them all. If, however, all of them will charge for your initial chat, you may want to save bucks by simply meeting with whichever lawyer has been most highly recommended or resume your search.

Once in the door, ask the following questions:

- *Are you a full-time attorney specializing in real estate transactions?* That's what you're looking for.

- *How long have you been practicing locally?* Real estate laws differ not only from state to state but also from community to community. You want a lawyer who is up-to-date on local laws, ordinances, and customs.

- *If I retain you to handle the sale of my house, what would you estimate the total charge to be?* Lawyers bill by the hour. Get both the lawyer's hourly rate and a "best guess" of how many hours will be spent representing you.

- *How much courtroom experience do you have?* Before your heart drops too far into your stomach, remember this: You are very unlikely to end up in court over the sale of your house. But on the outside chance that a buyer would ever want to sue you, it's good to have a lawyer with trial experience.

- *What is your record of wins and losses at trial?* You want a winner.

- *What are your strong points in pulling a sale together?* This question will give the lawyer a chance to show off a little, enumerating his or her skills. You can then determine if these skills match those that you're looking for in an attorney. At the very least, a lawyer should be able to prepare counteroffers that support your best interests; to prepare the counteroffer within the time frame demanded by the seller; to work within your time frame for closing the sale; and to prepare the closing statement.

- *What is your experience in canceling transactions?* Hire a lawyer who not only can help you secure a sale but also can get you out of one if you discover it's not in your best interest.

- *What special problems have you faced in real estate transactions and how were you able to resolve them?* As the lawyer responds, look for creativity in solving problems without resorting to costly lawsuits.

- *Explain the Seller's Disclosure of Property Condition Form to me. How do I use it and why?* You'll learn about the Seller's Disclosure of Property Condition Form later in this chapter. You ask this question merely to gauge the lawyer's knowledge of disclosure. If you seem to know more than the lawyer does, look for another attorney.

Finally, make sure that the lawyers you interview are licensed to practice in your state. This is not as ridiculous as it sounds. If you live somewhere in the middle of Nebraska, you have no problem. But suppose you live on the New Jersey side of the Delaware River, and the lawyer you hope to retain works in Pennsylvania. Make sure that lawyer can legally practice in New Jersey.

Who's the Boss?

Because you're paying cash for your lawyer's services, you clearly want to pay attention to any advice rendered. But remember, you're the boss. You know your situation best, and you have to decide whether to implement or reject the lawyer's advice.

Consider FSBOs William and Lisa Henry. Their house sat on the market for two months with no offers and few showings. As the new house they were having built neared completion, they started to panic at the idea of having to make two payments on two separate mortgages. Finally, they found a willing buyer.

The couple's lawyer thought they should reject the offer. It was way too low, he said. The couple needed to demand more earnest money and an earlier closing date. Oh, and they absolutely had to take their washer-dryer combo with them, even though the buyer asked that they leave it.

William and Lisa needed to sell their house and they felt they'd lose the buyer by following their lawyer's suggestions. They followed their own counsel and sold the house at a price everyone could live with.

Your Legal Rights

Most homesellers find their lawyers' advice sound, especially when it comes to representing their rights and responsibilities as sellers. Your lawyer will fill you in on these issues but, for now, here's the thumbnail version. You have the legal right to

- Sell your house without the use of an agent.

- Market your house at any price you choose.

- Sell your house at any price.

- Change your mind about selling it.

- Place a sign in your yard offering your house for sale, as long as the sign complies with local ordinances.

- Show your house to anyone you want.

- Refuse to show your house to certain persons. This can be tricky. If a buyer shows up at your door acting inappropriately, you can refuse to let him in. You can't refuse to let him in, however, because of the color of his skin . Or because he is a she. Or because she worships at a mosque instead of a church. Equal opportunity housing guidelines are discussed below.

- Sell your house to anyone you choose.

- Refuse to sell your house to a certain buyer. As with showing the house, you are allowed to refuse to sell your house to someone if you dislike his or her behavior. Consider the following example. A qualified buyer comes to your house and offers to purchase it at the price you're asking as long as you agree to fence in the backyard. Before you agree, you ask why a fenced-in-yard is so important to him. Your buyer says, "I have

four, count 'em, four, german shepherd watchdogs. Man, they bark all night long. No one is ever gonna hassle me. Took some time to get used to the noise, but now I can sleep right through it." That's good for the buyer but you know that constant barking will destroy the peaceful atmosphere of your neighborhood and inconvenience your friends and neighbors. You can refuse to sell to this buyer. You can't, however, refuse to sell to someone because he is using a Seeing Eye dog, for instance.

- Hire a brokerage firm and agent.

- Sue to terminate your listing agreement if you have just cause to be unhappy with your real estate agency's representation. Perhaps you feel that the agency has done nothing to market your house. Perhaps your agent doesn't return phone calls. Clearly, if you are fed up, your first recourse should be to see if you and the firm can mutually agree to cancel your contract. But, as a last resort, you can sue to get out of your agreement.

Your Legal Obligations

As a seller, you have both rights and responsibilities. You are obligated to

- Show your house, or allow it to be shown, but only at your convenience.

- Show your house to interested parties, and eventually sell it, without regard to race, color, religion, national origin, sex, or disability. In addition, you may not discriminate against families simply because they have young children or against a couple because they're elderly.

- Fulfill all the terms and conditions of the purchase agreement that has been signed by both you and the buyer. These terms usually include price, purchase of title insurance, an agreed-upon closing date, completion of a house inspection, and so forth.

- Show the buyer a signed Lead-Based Paint Disclosure Form, if your home was built before 1978, as well as a Seller Disclosure of Property Condition Form. These forms are discussed thoroughly later in this chapter.

- Leave your house in the condition it was in when you signed the purchase agreement.

- At closing, turn over the keys, automatic garage door openers, and other agreed-upon devices.

If you have hired a brokerage firm to represent you, you also must

- Pay an agreed-upon fee or commission upon the closing of your house.

- Allow the brokerage firm to market your house for the time agreed upon in the listing contract.

Let's Be Fair, Folks

The Federal Fair Housing Act and other laws mandate that you cannot discriminate against potential buyers because of their race, color, religion, sex, country of national origin, or disability. You also cannot refuse to sell to a family simply because some of its members are young children. Your state or municipality may also extend protection against discrimination to other groups, notably, homosexual partners.

If you ignore these laws, beware. People who feel victimized by discrimination can take several courses of action. They may file a complaint with the Department of Housing and Urban Development, demanding that you remedy any fair housing violation. They may also take court action, seeking actual damages, court costs, and unlimited punitive damages.

Other federal penalties can include fines of up to $50,000 for repeat offenders, punitive damages, and court costs.

Advertising without Discriminating

By now you may be thinking, "I'm no bigot. This doesn't concern me."

Beware though: Even the most tolerant people can run into unexpected legal problems if they are unaware of the laws governing for sale advertising in their area. Some

states deem unacceptable any reference to religious landmarks ("Across the street from St. Mary's Church") or racial landmarks ("Two blocks north of the Martin Luther King Jr. Memorial"). Advertising your property as the "perfect location for hikers, swimmers, and bikers" may be perceived by some municipalities as discriminating against the handicapped. Finally, many states disallow phrases such as "private community" because they seem to exclude certain classes.

Be safe. Protect yourself. Talk to your lawyer, local fair housing authority, or state civil rights commission to ensure that your ads don't inadvertently appear to discriminate against anyone.

The Fairness of Things

If you have any questions about fair housing laws, you can contact local housing resources boards, local human rights commissions, and state civil rights commissions. Or you can go straight to the feds.

Here's some contact information:

U.S. Dept. of Housing and Urban Development
Office of Fair Housing and Equal Opportunity
451 7th Street Southwest
Washington, DC 20410
800-424-8590

HUD National Housing Hotline
800-669-9777, TDD 800-927-9275

Disclosure

Virtually every seller in this country has to provide potential buyers with a Disclosure of Property Condition Form (see Appendix D). Owners of houses built before 1978 must also produce a Lead-Based Paint Disclosure Form (see Appendix B).

You can get these forms from your lawyer or agent. If you have any questions, do not hesitate to contact these professionals for information on the right way to respond to questions posed in these documents.

Seller's Disclosure of Property Condition Form

Most states now require some form of seller disclosure of the condition of the property marketed. The form protects both seller and buyer, in that the buyer, by freely signing the form, acknowledges the condition of the house and can't come back to sue you for the expense of repairing any of the defects listed on the form. The form should cover the overall condition of your house as well as the condition of appliances and components.

Overall condition. This section of your disclosure form covers what you'd expect: basement/foundation, roof, well and pump, septic systems, sewer systems, heating systems, plumbing and electrical systems, and groundwater contamination. You may not know, however, that it also covers the presence of dangerous substances such as asbestos and radon.

Asbestos, which is often found insulating furnace and duct work in older houses, is now a suspected carcinogen. Radon is an odorless, colorless gas (you only learn of its presence by testing for it) known to cause serious health problems, including lung cancer. Clearly, the house's new owners would want to know about the presence of these substances.

Appliances and components. You'll need to tell any prospective buyer what you know about your ranges, dishwashers, refrigerators, alarm systems, pool heaters, wall liners, sump pumps, fireplaces, and chimneys. If the appliance or component does not stay with the house as a result of the sale, its condition is of no consequence. However, if it is to stay, you need to be as accurate as possible in your assessment of its condition.

As noted in chapter 3, you may have had a home inspection performed yourself. If so, you should know of any flaws in your house. But if you live in an area where custom dictates that the seller pay for an inspection of your home, you may honestly not yet know of certain problems. In this case, simply use the word *unknown*. This will alert the buyer that an inspection is necessary.

Here's an example. You're filling out the Property Condition Disclosure Form. You indicate that the roof is 20 years old. To your knowledge, it doesn't leak. Then you reach a question asking you to describe the condition of the roof shingles. Because you've not been crawling around up there for a while, you simply reply, "Unknown." This word will alert the buyer that the roof should be inspected.

Lead-Based Paint Disclosure Form

Because exposure to lead-based paint may place children at risk of lead poisoning, you need to disclose to the buyer any information you have on the presence of such paint in your house. This only applies if your house was built prior to 1978.

The disclosure form asks whether you know of any lead-based paint in the house and whether you have reports on the issue that the buyer may inspect. The buyer must acknowledge on the disclosure form that he or she has received copies of any information and/or reports that you have available. The buyer then has the opportunity to conduct a risk assessment or inspection to determine how to rid the house of lead-based paint.

GET THE LEAD OUT

Children can become ill and die from exposure to lead-based paints. If you have any questions at all about the presence of this substance in your house, contact:

National Lead Information Clearing House
800-724-LEAD
Government Printing Office
202-512-1800
Stock #055-000-00507-9
EPA Pamphlet & Rule
919-558-0335

Honesty Is the Best Policy

You must fill out disclosure forms as completely and honestly as you can. Otherwise, you run the real risk of lawsuits. Don't fudge anything.

Jane Door, reading her seller disclosure form, came to a section that read, "Physical problems: Any known settling, flooding, drainage, or grading problems." She chose to note only that her house had a "weeping wall tie." A more accurate response would have been, "The house is built on a high water table."

The house was eventually sold. After a major rainstorm, the new owner discovered three inches of water in the basement. He learned of the high water table afterward, when he commissioned an inspection of the foundation. He sued Jane big time and won.

Don't put yourself—or your buyer—in this position. It's just not worth it.

WELL, WE TRIED

In this section, you've read some general guidelines concerning the Seller's Disclosure of Property Condition Form and the Lead-Based Paint Disclosure Form. Remember, these are general guidelines only. You must check with your real estate agent or lawyer to be sure you've filled out these forms properly and to see if your state or municipality mandates any other disclosures.

Agency Laws

In chapter 2 we discussed how you hire a broker. In days past, all agents and brokers worked for the seller because the seller paid the commission.

All that has changed in recent years. In addition to traditional seller's agents, you may now work with agents who represent the buyer, or even agents who try to represent both parties. Let's take a look at buyer's brokers and dual agents to see how your relationship with them may affect the sale of your house.

Buyer's Brokers and Agents

You've already learned about your agent's responsibilities to you. Now let's turn the scenario around.

Brokers have begun representing buyers, too. If you deal with buyer's brokers, remember that their primary loyalty is to their client—the buyer.

In chapter 2 we said your broker owes you confidentiality, loyalty, disclosure, accounting of cash flow, and obedience to your lawful instruction. Buyer's brokers provide the other side with these same services.

Always keep this in mind with buyer's brokers, especially when it comes to disclosure. If you should happen to say to a buyer's broker, "Well, we'd be inclined to accept this $180,000 offer if we had to, but we're going to counter with $185,000 just to see if the buyer will come up a bit," the broker must report this information back to the client.

Conversely, buyer's brokers cannot reveal to you any information regarding, for instance, how motivated the client is to buy your house, what price the client may "come up to" during counteroffers, and so on.

Dual Agents

Some states allow dual agency, a situation in which a single real estate agent represents both buyer and seller. Any real estate broker must receive the permission of both parties before commencing this type of relationship, in which the buyer and seller are supposed to benefit equally.

Dual agents back away from the responsibilities of loyalty and disclosure to each party to maintain the confidentiality of both the seller and the buyer. They take a neutral stance, refusing to represent one party to a greater degree than the other.

Ask!

An agent representing a buyer is usually legally required to tell you so. Ditto for a salesperson hoping to act as a dual agent. However, people are human and sometimes they forget to reveal this information. Less reputable salespeople may "forget" on purpose. Of course, such deliberate forgetfulness is illegal in most places but very, very hard to prove. If you ever feel that you have been duped, talk to a qualified attorney. And to avoid legal unpleasantries, ask agents who call or walk through your door who they represent and tailor your relationship with them accordingly.

Bottom-Line Thinking

In this chapter, you were clued in on:

- How to find a real estate lawyer

- Your rights as a seller

- Your obligations as a seller

- Fair housing laws

- The disclosure forms you must sign

- How to deal with buyer's agents, buyer's brokers, and dual agents

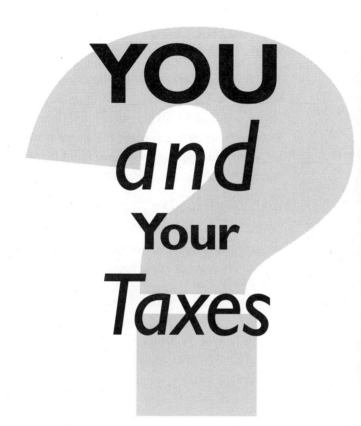

YOU and Your Taxes

CHAPTER FIVE

People who win more than $600 on Wheel of Fortune *must* report their earnings to the IRS. You're probably going to make more than $600 on the sale of your house, so you're undoubtedly worried about the tax bite.

Want to solve the puzzle? Unlike those big-winning folks on *Wheel of Fortune* you are going to make out like a bandit under new tax laws.

Read this chapter and you'll get a clue about:

- How to figure your profit on the sale of your house

- How to determine what earnings are tax exempt

- Estate tax on the sale of a residence

- The tax consequences of selling at a loss

THE BIBLE THIS AIN'T

You're not reading the Bible here. You're reading a how-to book for clueless people. The point?

In this chapter, we've provided you with some very general tax guidelines. You absolutely, positively, must talk to your accountant to determine the effect tax laws will have on the sale of your house.

Figuring Your Profit on the Sale

The difference between what you bought your house for and what you sell it for is called *profit*. Nice word, that one. The value of your house is likely to have increased if the real estate market has improved since you purchased the place or if you improved the house in any way.

In short, the IRS will only tax you on profit earned because of a strengthening real estate market. It won't charge you if the value of your house has risen because of improvements.

Let's say you bought your house 15 years ago for $90,000. Your closing costs totaled $3,400. Since taking up residence, you've spent $30,000 for a family room addition and $10,000 to remodel the kitchen.

Special Assessments

If you have incurred a "special assessment" charge, such as for the improvement of sidewalks, street lights, and the like, you may earn additional tax credits. Whatever you paid for these amenities can be included in the overall cost of your house, right next to purchase price, closing costs, and improvements. These assessments increase the total price paid for your house, and the IRS won't charge you if the value of your house has risen because of these special assessments.

Now it's time to sell. You accepted an offer of $240,000, and shelled out $22,000 for real estate commissions and the closing costs you assumed. With these figures in hand, you can begin to determine your profit and your likely tax bill.

Start with the cost of the house—purchase price, closing costs, and improvements.

Purchase price	$ 90,000
Closing costs	3,400
Improvements	40,000
Total	$133,400

Follow up by determining your adjusted sales price—or the money you're making from the sale of the house, minus the amount it cost you to sell it. In the above scenario, the figures would run this way:

Sales price	$240,000
Cost of selling (including commission)	22,000
Adjusted sales price (price minus costs)	$218,000

Now it's time for you to figure out your taxable profit. To do this, subtract the amount you spent to buy and improve the house from your adjusted sales price.

Adjusted sales price	$218,000
Cost to buy/improve	133,400
Taxable profit	$ 84,600

Based on this scenario, how much do you owe the IRS? Lucky you. Quite possibly not a dime.

Tax Provisions Affecting the Sale of Your House

Laws enacted in 1997 offer substantial benefits to taxpayers selling their principal residences. Let's take a look at some of them.

Keep the Receipts

As you know by now, the IRS will not charge you for a profit made for the sale of your house based on any improvements you made to it.

But what are you going to say? "Please don't penalize us, Mr. Auditor. We know that we bought the house 50 years ago for $70,000, and sold it on Thursday for $900,000, but really, we didn't make $830,000. We only made an $800,000 profit because we spent the other $30,000 to add a den. You should see it! It's really quite homey."

Those nice folks at the IRS are not just going to take your word for it. You must keep the receipts and canceled checks for any work you paid for on your house. Ditto for any special assessments you have had to pay.

For federal tax purposes (your state requirements may differ), you should maintain records showing the purchase price, closing costs, and any improvements to your residence for as long as you own the property, and for an additional three years after the sale.

Under the new laws, married taxpayers filing joint returns do not have to pay taxes on the first $500,000 profit earned from the sale of their homes. Single persons, and anyone else who doesn't file a joint return, can enjoy the first $250,000 in profit tax free.

There are three standards that you must meet in order to qualify for these tax breaks. They are:

- *Ownership.* You must have owned your home for periods of at least two years of the five years preceding the sale.

- *Use.* You must have used the property as your principal residence for periods of at least two years of the five years preceding the sale.

- *Waiting period.* You cannot have utilized this exclusion for any sale during the last two years.

Obviously, most homesellers are thrilled to death with these exemptions. They're also happy that new laws don't require them to spend their profits on a new house to receive the tax break.

You may get a tax break even if you fail to meet some of the "two-year" provisions listed above. If your company demands that you relocate, or if health concerns mandate that you move to a warmer climate, you may be able to claim a percentage of the exclusion, although not the whole shebang.

The laws are fairly straightforward, but special consideration should be given to the following scenarios:

- *My spouse died.* You may claim up to a $500,000 profit, tax free, on the sale of your house if you choose to sell it within one year of the death of your spouse. If you sell later, you may only claim a $250,000 profit exclusion (unless you're remarried and filing jointly).

- *If you sell like a bandit.* Say you bought a $75,000 house on some prime property near a highway. Megamart approaches you some years later saying "Hi, married homeowners filing jointly! We need this land for our new store. We're offering $750,000 for your half-acre." Remember, people filing jointly are only tax-exempt for the first $500,000 in profit. Single persons can only make $250,000 before they have to start paying taxes on their earnings. In this scenario, the extraordinarily lucky married homeowners would have to pay capital gains taxes on $175,000 of their profit.

- *If you sell at a loss.* Unfortunately, under new laws, sale losses remain non-deductible.

- *I inherited this monster.* Rules going into effect currently exempt $650,000 of property value on estate sales (not necessarily real estate— check with your tax adviser). The amount exempted from estate sales and

farm sales will increase by $25,000 each year beginning in 2000, to a total possible exemption of $1.3 million.

Reporting Your Sale

Once you've sold your house, the party in charge of the closing (usually a title or closing company, a lawyer, or a lender) will prepare an affidavit for you to sign at the closing table declaring that you owe no taxes on the sale, and that's that. However, if you don't fit the criteria for the exemption (explained earlier), then you simply report the amount of taxes on the schedule for capital gains attached to your Form 1040 personal income tax return.

Bottom-Line Thinking

In this chapter, you got a clue about:

- How to determine the actual profit on the sale of your house

- How much you can profit, tax free, from the sale of your house

- Selling your house at a loss

- How tax laws apply to estate sales

- How to report your sale to the IRS

READY, Set, SELL!

CHAPTER SIX

Now that you've decided to place your house on the market, you're undoubtedly wondering how to price it and how to prepare it so potential buyers see it in its best light. If you're not wondering about these issues, you should be.

Read this chapter and you'll get a clue about:

- How to price your house

- How to read and interpret a comparative market analysis

- How to conduct your own research

- How to prepare your house for sale

What's Your House Worth?

Your house is worth exactly what your "best buyer" is willing to pay for it. One buyer may offer $160,000. Your best buyer may offer $175,000. Your house, therefore, is worth 175 grand.

BUYERS PINCH PENNIES

Buyers generally look for the lowest-priced house in a given range.

People who have between $120,000 and $130,000 to spend on a house are clearly not going to buy a $57,000 starter home. But say they find two houses in their price range, both of which meet their needs. One is priced at $122,000; the other at $127,000. Unless the more expensive house has some outstanding feature that merits spending an extra five grand, these buyers will likely purchase the $122,000 property.

Keep this phenomenon in mind when you determine the price of your house.

You can price your two-bedroom bungalow for $90,000 if you want to, even though all the comparable places in the area are selling for $75,000.

"Oh," you think, "I'll price my bungalow at $90,000. I can always come down to $75,000."

Think again. A buyer with only $75,000 to spend is going to offer to buy a bungalow comparable to yours marketed at $78,000. That buyer figures it will be easier to get those sellers to come down $3,000 than to get you to come down $15,000.

Overpriced houses scare off buyers. These properties face other problems, too. Their agents are unenthusiastic about trying to sell them. Cooperating real estate agents and buyer's brokers won't bother showing these houses to buyers. Buyers aren't stupid, and the ones who do tour the place will leave shaking their heads. Eventually, these properties just sit on the market. And the longer a house sits on the market, the harder it is to sell.

Conversely, a competitive price draws buyers. Its agent will show the place with more enthusiasm, an enthusiasm that rubs off on both potential buyers and cooperating agents. It gets shown more often, and sells faster.

FSBOs Take Note

Competitive pricing is always important but never more so than in a FSBO sale. Because buyers are generally inconvenienced working with a FSBO, and because they know you're saving big bucks on real estate commissions, they expect your house to have more amenities and be offered at a better price than comparable properties on the market.

Why Sellers Overprice

Now that you know how important it is to price your house competitively, you may wonder why you see so many inflated price tags. Here are a few reasons:

- *Ego.* Sellers take pride in their houses, especially if they've spent time and money to remodel or decorate. To them, it just "feels" nicer than any other house on the block. Therefore, they price it higher.

- *Those people down the street practically gave their house away.* The desire to sell at a good price has led many homeowners to indulge in false logic. The faulty reasoning goes like this: "Sure, I know that all the other comparable houses in the neighborhood are going for $75,000, but I need to gross $90,000 on this sale so, therefore, my house must be worth $90,000. Everybody else is pricing way too low." Get real, and start thinking, "Yeah, I need $90,000, but I'm only going to gross $75,000 for the sale. Now how can I make the other $15,000?"

- *Market trends don't affect me.* Let's call this the "charmed circle theory." Nothing truly bad can ever happen to you because you're, well, you. This isn't the first time in your life (go on, admit it) you've believed that bad stuff can be going on all around you and it isn't going to affect you one whit. You think you're in a charmed circle of individuals who just don't get roughed up by life the way the rest of us do. Trust us here, though. If marketing trends in your area indicate that house prices have dropped 10 percent over the last two years, it's not just your neighbors who suffer when they put their place on the block. It's you, too—no matter how lucky you think you are.

- *Misinformation.* An unethical real estate agent may have inflated the price of your house because he or she wants the listing. (You're human. Who are you going to hire? An agent who says he can sell your house for $180,000 or an agent who says she can sell it for $200,000?) Or you spoke with the owners of a comparable property, one listed at $190,000, who said they got what they wanted for the sale of their home. Beware of taking such statements to heart. Maybe all those homeowners wanted was to unload their property quickly, and even though it listed for $190,000, they gladly accepted $173,000.

- *You overestimate the appreciation.* Houses increase in value when the economy booms in their areas. This is called *appreciation.* If you live in such a market, terrific. But many homesellers have mistakenly thought that because houses in the posh end of town are appreciating at a rate of 5 percent a year, the price of their houses, on the working-class side of the city, must be rising at the same rate. This is not necessarily true.

- *Recapture the price of improvements.* Sellers often mistakenly think that when it comes time to sell they can recapture the cost of all the improvements they've made to their house. Not true. With the exception of kitchen improvements, sellers rarely make back the full price of installing amenities, whether they be new roofs, new pools, or anything else you can think of.

Pricing Your House to Sell

"Okay, okay," you think, "I'm not going to get greedy with this sale. I'll price my house competitively. I just don't know how."

Have no fear. There are many ways you can determine you home's best sale price. They include: talking to real estate agents, hiring an appraiser, and heading off to the county courthouse yourself to see what comparable houses have sold for. The Internet can also provide a wealth of information to assist you in pricing your house for sale.

Contacting Agents

After touring your house, your agent will research the sale prices of comparable homes in your area and the list prices of houses currently on the market. Your agent will check out only houses that are very, very much like yours—those that sit in the same neighborhood or a similar one; those of the same style (one story, two story, etc.); and those with similar square footage.

After comparing location, style, and size, the agent begins to compare other features: the number of bedrooms and baths; the size of the garage; the age of the house; the privacy of the lot; and other amenities such as the presence of a formal dining room, a finished basement, and so forth.

The agent puts all this information together in a report called a *comparative market analysis,* or CMA. This document helps you and your agent determine the price range in which your house should sell.

Expired Listings in the CMA

Don't be surprised if the CMA prepared by your real estate agent includes a few *expired listings,* or homes that failed to sell during their owners' terms of contract with brokerage firms. Maybe no one bought these places because they were priced too high. Your real estate agent will include them in the CMA to warn you of the dangers of getting greedy.

Comparative Market Analysis

Owner's Name and Address: _____

# Bedrooms	_____
# Baths	_____
Family Room	_____
Rec Room	_____
Age	_____
Garage (attached/detached)	_____
Lot Size	_____
Central Air	_____
Terms	_____
Square Feet	_____
Remarks	_____

Features/Comments: _____
_____
_____

Sold Properties	**#1**	**#2**	**#3**
# Bedrooms	_____	_____	_____
# Baths	_____	_____	_____
Family Room	_____	_____	_____
Rec Room	_____	_____	_____
Age	_____	_____	_____
Garage (attached/detached)	_____	_____	_____
Lot Size	_____	_____	_____
Central Air	_____	_____	_____
Terms	_____	_____	_____
Days on Market	_____	_____	_____
Square Feet	_____	_____	_____
List Price	_____	_____	_____
Sales Price	_____	_____	_____
Sales Price per Square Foot	_____	_____	_____

Competing Properties   #1   #2   #3

Bedrooms   _____   _____   _____
Baths   _____   _____   _____
Family Room   _____   _____   _____
Rec Room   _____   _____   _____
Age   _____   _____   _____
Garage (attached/detached)   _____   _____   _____
Lot Size   _____   _____   _____
Central Air   _____   _____   _____
Terms   _____   _____   _____
Days on Market   _____   _____   _____
Square Feet   _____   _____   _____
List Price   _____   _____   _____
List Price per Square Foot   _____   _____   _____
Sales Price When Sells   _____   _____   _____

Expired Properties   #1   #2   #3

Bedrooms   _____   _____   _____
Baths   _____   _____   _____
Family Room   _____   _____   _____
Rec Room   _____   _____   _____
Age   _____   _____   _____
Garage (attached/detached)   _____   _____   _____
Lot Size   _____   _____   _____
Central Air   _____   _____   _____
Terms   _____   _____   _____
Days on Market   _____   _____   _____
Square Feet   _____   _____   _____
List Price   _____   _____   _____
List Price per Square Foot   _____   _____   _____
Remarks   _____   _____   _____

Recommended Listing Price $ _____
Anticipated Selling Price Range $ _____ to $ _____
Prepared by: _____
Date: _____

CMAs Everywhere

Remember, by now you should have whittled your list of potential real estate agents to three. You have asked each to deliver a listing presentation to you. This presentation will include a marketing plan and a CMA. So you may end up with as many as three CMAs. This is terrific. You want as much information as possible before deciding at what price to market your house.

Do Your Own Research

FSBOs often perform their own market research. Sometimes sellers represented by brokers do, too—just to double check their agents' work.

If you want to put together your own CMA, start by visiting your county courthouse. Find the office where these sales records are housed—usually the tax assessor's office, treasurer's office, or recorder of deed's office.

Remember, your goal is to find sales of houses that are comparable to yours. Look for properties:

- In your neighborhood, or as close by as possible

- Built in the same style as yours (a one-story ranch, a two-story colonial, for example)

- The same size as yours in terms of square feet

- Including the same number of bedrooms as yours

- With the same size garage as yours

- Boasting the same type of amenities as your house, for example, decks, patios, a screened-in-porch, Jacuzzi, pool, or sauna

Note the sale price of each house. Select three or four most like yours to establish a price range. If you're a FSBO, determine a reasonable price for your house and contact your consulting real estate agent to see if you're on track.

Get an Appraisal

If you're a FSBO, have a professional appraiser look at your house. It will likely cost you between $200 and $400, but it will be cash well spent. The average buyer will not question a certified professional's unbiased report on the value of a house. It's such a sound psychological tool that even some sellers who have contracted with real estate agents have decided to hire appraisers.

Estimated Seller's Net Return Form

Once you and your agent have determined at what price you hope to market your house, the agent will probably prepare for you an Estimated Seller's Net Return Form, detailing how much you will walk away with after your mortgage is satisfied and you pay any closing costs mandated.

Remember, this is an estimate only. Your agent cannot know what your house will eventually sell for.

Estimate of Seller's Net Return

Seller _____ Closing Date _____

Address _____

Based on a Selling Price of $ _____

Existing Mortgage	$ _____
Second Mortgage	$ _____
Property Taxes (Prorated):	
Previous year	$ _____
Current year	$ _____
Documentary Stamps	$ _____
Interest to Date of Closing	$ _____
Recording Fee	$ _____
Brokerage Fee (___ %)	$ _____
Attorney Fees	$ _____
Abstract/Title Insurance	$ _____
Special Assessments	$ _____
Inspection, termite	$ _____
Inspection, well and septic	$ _____
Inspection, miscellaneous:	
_____	$ _____
_____	$ _____
_____	$ _____
Buyer's Loan Discount Points	$ _____
Alimony	$ _____
Child Support	$ _____
Miscellaneous expenses:	
_____	$ _____
_____	$ _____
_____	$ _____

TOTAL SELLER'S COST	– $ _____
ESCROW ACCOUNT BALANCE (Estimate)	+ $ _____
ESTIMATED NET RETURN TO SELLER	$ _____

Preparing Your House For Sale

You've compiled a CMA or had an appraiser place a value on your house. Now it's time to ready the place for sale. Make no mistake: In addition to competitive pricing, cleanliness and cosmetics sell a property.

Next to Godliness

To sell your house, the place must look clean, smell clean, and be clean. Drag out the mops, brooms, and vacuums; stock up on wood soap and polish; and don't forget the glass cleaner.

You may not be naturally neat. You may, in fact, feel perfectly happy with some bread crumbs and peanut butter and jelly splotches on your kitchen counter. Remember this though: Potential buyers cringe at this type of mess. They're not comfortable with PB&J stains on your counter. They're only comfortable with PB&J stains on their own counters. There is a huge difference.

Here's a general guide to preparing and cleaning each room:

- *Front door.* Sweep off the stoop. Polish your doorknob. Make sure any glass on the door sparkles—no streaks. Stick a plant out there. You want your front-door area to look as inviting as possible.

- *Foyer/Hallway.* Remove clutter. Mop or vacuum the floor. Dust the molding and floor boards. Clean out hall closets—a clean closet looks more spacious. Dust or wash the closet shelves.

- *Living room.* This may be the room with the nice furniture that nobody ever uses. (You all hang out in the den—you know, the room with the beat-up furniture that everybody uses.) Stand at the doorway and pretend to be a buyer. See whether this room has gotten dusty from lack of use. Wash the windows. Wash and iron, or dry-clean, the curtains. Vacuum.

- *Dining room.* You may use your dining room table as storage. Get rid of all the junk stored there and place a fresh tablecloth on the table. Top it

Owners Checklist

The following is a checklist, detailed to help you make an inspection and repair record as you prepare your house for sale.

Checklist for Landscaping

Lawn

Lawn in good condition —

Grass mowed —

Edges trimmed around

  walks —

  driveways —

  trees —

  fences —

Trees

Dead branches pruned —

Dead trees removed —

Plantings

Dead shrubs removed —

Dead shrubs replaced —

Overgrown shrubs pruned —

Checklist for Exterior

House

Recently painted —

Free of flaking paint —

Gutters free of rust —

Gutters recently painted —

Exterior lights operating —

Missing shingles replaced —

Doorbell working —

Exterior brass polished —

Windows

  Cracked panes replaced —

  Trim recently painted —

  Work freely —

Driveway

Resurfaced —

Potholes patched —

Recently sealed —

Pebbles smoothed —

Pebbles weeded —

Patios

Wood stained or painted —

Fencing secure —

No standing water —

Checklist for Garage

Excess storage removed —

Floor swept and clear —

Tools stored neatly —

Paint supplies stored —

Garden tools on hooks —

Workbench area well lit —

Light fixtures operating —

Oil spots removed from floor —

Door operating —

Door lubricated —

Cracked window panes replaced —

Electric door opener operable —

Checklist for Kitchen

Sink free of cracks —

Sink free of stains —

No dripping faucets —

Refrigerator defrosted —

Appliances in working order —

Missing floor tiles replaced —

Walls free of grease stains —

Countertops cleared

Pantry and cabinets

  Neatly arranged —

  Hardware replaced —

  Excess storage removed —

Checklist for Living Room

Cracks in ceiling repaired ___
Cracks in walls repaired ___
Water stains covered ___
Walls recently painted ___
Wallpaper repaired ___
Woodwork repainted ___
Windows repaired ___
Windows washed ___
Curtains washed and ironed ___
Floor refinished and waxed ___
Carpets cleaned and secure ___
Furniture positioned to show space ___
Large pieces stored elsewhere ___

Checklist for Dining Room

Cracks in ceiling repaired ___
Cracks in walls repaired ___
Water stains covered ___
Walls recently painted ___
Wallpaper repaired ___
Woodwork repainted ___
Windows repaired ___
Windows washed ___
Curtains washed and ironed ___
Floor refinished and waxed ___
Carpets cleaned and secure ___
Furniture positioned to show space ___
Large pieces stored elsewhere ___

Checklist for Family Room

Cracks in ceiling repaired ___
Cracks in walls repaired ___
Water stains covered ___
Walls recently painted ___
Wallpaper repaired ___
Woodwork repainted ___
Windows repaired ___
Windows washed ___
Curtains washed and ironed ___

Floor refinished and waxed ___
Carpets cleaned and secure ___
Furniture positioned to show space ___
Large pieces stored elsewhere ___

Checklist for Bedroom   #1 #2 #3

	#1	#2	#3
Cracks in ceiling repaired	___	___	___
Cracks in walls repaired	___	___	___
Water stains covered	___	___	___
Walls recently painted	___	___	___
Wallpaper repaired	___	___	___
Woodwork repainted	___	___	___
Windows repaired	___	___	___
Windows washed			
Curtains washed and ironed	___	___	___
Floor refinished and waxed	___	___	___
Carpets cleaned and secure	___	___	___
Furniture moved to show space	___	___	___
Large pieces stored elsewhere	___	___	___

Checklist for Bathroom   #1 #2 #3

	#1	#2	#3
Sink stains removed	___	___	___
Leaky faucets repaired	___	___	___
Stains removed from grout	___	___	___
All joints caulked	___	___	___
Broken or missing tiles replaced	___	___	___
All fixtures operating	___	___	___
Recently painted	___	___	___
Wallpaper repaired	___	___	___
Floors cleaned	___	___	___
New shower curtain	___	___	___

Checklist for Entrance Hall

Doorbell operating ___
Door recently painted ___
Door brass polished ___
Hardware operating ___
Hinges oiled ___
Broken hinges replaced ___

Entryway lights operating	___	No evidence of water penetration ___
Floors cleaned	___	Dampness removed ___
Rugs cleaned and secure	___	Cold water pipes covered ___
Cracks in ceiling repaired	___	Dehumidifier installed ___
Cracks in walls repaired	___	Sump pump installed ___
Wallpaper repaired	___	No musty odors ___
Walls recently repainted	___	Drains cleared ___
Windows repaired	___	Furnace cleaned ___
Windows washed	___	Storage neatly arranged ___
Closet cleaned out	___	Floor cleaned ___
Closet light operating	___	Light fixtures operating ___
		Laundry area clean and light ___
Checklist for Basement		Stairway clear ___
Cracks in ceiling repaired	___	Handrail secure ___
Cracks in walls repaired	___	

off with a vase of fresh flowers. Wash the windows and the curtains. Wash the crystal in the hutch. Clean the chandelier. Vacuum the rug or polish the floor.

- *Kitchen*. Clear the counters. Scrub them thoroughly. Scrub the walls and counter doors. Clean your stove's surface and its nooks and crannies. Organize the cupboards and wash the shelves. Apply fresh shelf paper. Wash the windows. Scrub the floor.

- *Family room or study*. Clear the clutter. Wash the windows. Vacuum the carpet or scrub the floor. Wash the curtains. Dust.

- *Bedrooms*. Clean the closets, putting some space between each hanger. Hang clothes of similar length together. Wash the shelves, leaving some storage space empty on each. Keep part of the floor visible. Wash the bedroom windows. Wash the bedspread or have it dry-cleaned.

- *Bathrooms*. Get rid of clutter. Bleach any stains in the sink, tub, or shower. Clean glass shower doors. Get rid of any mildew. Clean the cosmetic

or perfume bottles on view. Dust the towel bars. Wash the towels. Wash the throw rugs. Scrub the floor.

- *Basement.* Clear the clutter. Arrange any stored items. Get rid of any damp or musty odors—hire a professional to help if necessary.

- *Garage.* Get rid of clutter. Hang up garden utensils and other tools. Sweep cobwebs from the walls and the ceiling. Sweep and wash the floor.

- *Back and front yards.* Stand across the street and look at your house and the property. How does it look? You may need to mow the lawn, trim tree branches, or remove dead trees and shrubs.

- *House exterior.* While you're standing across the street, look at the exterior of your house. If you're unhappy with its appearance, wash the windows, polish exterior brass, clean out the gutters, and clean and sweep the patio.

Once your house begins to sparkle, start to think of general cosmetics. Walk through each room again. If the paint or wallpaper is scuffed or faded, touch it up or replace it. Replace broken hardware, torn screens, and cracked or broken windows. Repair ceiling and wall cracks. Refinish wood floors, if necessary. Secure stairway runners. Replace washers in leaking faucets.

None of these chores will take you more than a few hours and a few bucks to fix. However, homesellers do run into larger expenses, incurred for both cosmetics and necessary repairs.

There's not really an easy way to ask this question, but do you perhaps have unusual tastes? If you love your purple shag wall-to-wall carpeting because it so nicely compliments your orange walls, more power to you. You should decorate in a style that makes you happy and comfortable.

But remember, you're putting your house on the market. Not everyone may appreciate this bold color scheme, and buyers have a notoriously poor ability to look beyond decor. You don't want to lose a sale because a potential buyer leaves your

house muttering, "There's no way we're buying a purple house, Harry." Consider repainting, and replacing the rug for a more neutral look.

You also may face structural problems. You may know you need a new roof or new heating system. You have a choice. You can either fix these now for a smoother sale or expect to come down in the price of your house. If the place needs a $5,000 roof job, savvy homebuyers will demand that you either fix it before you leave or drop the price of your house to cover their fixing it after closing.

What Else to Do?

You've cleaned and spruced up your house, but there are a few additional things you need to consider buying and doing to prepare your house for sale.

Have the place inspected. Your buyer will probably not buy the house without a home inspection. Who actually pays for it though, is up for grabs. In many areas it is customary for the buyer to pay for this service, but you may want to have it performed ahead of time—and pay for it yourself—to secure a quicker sale. Remember, if you do pay to have it inspected, make sure to put the results in your house book, which is discussed in chapter 3.

Buy a home warranty. You know all about warranties. You can't swing a dead cat in an electronics store these days without hitting a warrantied product. Your computer. Your large-screen TV. Your dishwasher.

They all come with either store or manufacturer's warranties that basically state: "If something goes wrong with this product within a certain time frame, we'll either repair or replace it for you for free."

Home warranties are no different. They usually cover the buyer for a year if, say, the roof should cave in. The buyer will usually demand that you pay for this insurance. But don't get too nervous, it usually costs less than $400.

Some homeowners may choose to buy this warranty after the home inspection but before securing an offer. They feel it makes the house more marketable. However,

buyers often like to decide for themselves which warranty they want you to buy. So you may want to wait until you have a firm offer.

Call your bank. As a courtesy, contact the bank that holds your current mortgage. Tell your banker that your have placed your house on the market. But don't worry about getting into all the financial specifics. Your escrow agent, title company, or attorney will call your banker to discuss current loan balances, home equity loans, and liens on the property, and to get instructions for paying them off.

Bottom-Line Thinking

By now, you should have a clue about:

- The dangers of overpricing your house

- How to price your house competitively

- What a comparative market analysis is and how to do one yourself, if you choose

- How to prepare your house for sale

LIFE on the MARKET

CHAPTER SEVEN

Congratulations! You're officially on the market. Well, maybe not you, but certainly your house.

It took a lot of prep work to get here—everything from choosing the right agent to cleaning out the gunk from under the refrigerator. You thought that work was hard, and you're right. It was. But nothing in your experience has prepared you for the out-and-out stress of strangers poking around your house.

In this chapter you'll learn how to survive the stampede (or complete lack thereof) of would-be buyers. You'll get a clue about:

- Average selling times

- How you and your agent set appointments, show the house, and follow up with prospects

- Handling buyer objections

- What to do if your house isn't selling

Expect Stress

Selling a house takes time. You know that. But the period between putting your house on the block and closing may seem more like "hard time." Life on the market isn't easy. You have to keep your house spotless, making the beds each day, doing the dishes each day, cleaning the bathrooms. If you and your family are used to a busy, more casual—OK, sloppy, not to put too fine a point on it—lifestyle, this new cleaning regime can grate all around.

Then there's the need to leave the house at a moment's notice, whenever a prospect feels like stopping by. If you've hired an agent to represent you in the sale, you probably don't want to be around when that agent shows the house. There's something unnerving about seeing other people poking their heads into your closets. You'd rather go out for coffee, leaving them in the capable hands of your salesperson. Your agent may even insist you make yourself scarce, fearing you'll reveal too much of your motivation to the buyer. If buyers know you need to be out of the house Thursday, they have a definite advantage in negotiations.

If you're a FSBO, expect an even more substantial disruption of your life. In addition to keeping the house gleaming, you'll likely have to leave work at times to run home and show the place. And weekends? Forget 'em. You'll be holding open houses and waiting by the phone, hoping for a visit or a call from your dream buyer.

How long do you have to live this way? For as long as it takes to sell your house. If you operate in a sound seller's market, you may get lucky and close within 90 days. If you live in a weak market, expect to wait six months, a year, or longer. And don't kick back too much the first time you get an offer. Don't stop advertising and don't let your house fall from its pristine state.

An unlovely truth about homeselling: Offers fall through. The transferee's new job vanishes. The prospects can't get financing or they simply change their minds.

Prepare for this unhappy contingency. Keep the For Sale sign planted in your front lawn. Keep the ads running. Keep answering the phone.

When They Come Knocking . . .

In chapter 3, FSBOs learned all about setting appointments with buyers. But what if you're contracting with a real estate agent to represent your house? You assume the responsibility of making it as easy as possible for the agent to show the place. Also, help your salesperson rope in buyers when you can.

Ask your agent to leave a stack of business cards with you. Here's why. Some curious folks are likely just to knock on your door, drawn by the broker's yard sign. Don't let them in. You don't know who they are, what their motives are, or whether they financially qualify to purchase your house. Instead, give the buyer one of your agent's business cards, and take the buyer's name and number. Call your agent with the information.

Lie!

You know by now that if buyers just stop by your house without an appointment, you shouldn't let them in. You don't know if they are qualified to buy the house. You don't know if they are serious buyers or Sunday window-shoppers. You don't even know if—heaven forbid—they are robbers.

But what are you going to say? "Naaah. This how-to book for clueless people told me not to let you in. 'Fraid you gotta talk to my agent."

Completely turning away a potential customer is never a good move.

Instead, you should beg off with a little fib. Say you're very sorry but that you're running late for an extremely important appointment. If you're clearly not running out to any such appointment—if the buyers catch you in your pj's or robe, for example—start coughing a lot and claim a terrible cold. Then give them one of your agent's cards.

Normally, buyers won't just show up at your house. They'll call your agent for an appointment to tour the property. Your agent will call to inform you of the showing date and time. Cooperating agents who have buyers interested in your house will either call you or call your agent.

Before you list your house, your agent will talk to you about the possibility of using a lockbox or a key-safe system, so that salespeople can show the place when you're not around.

The system works like this. Your house keys are locked in a box that hangs from your front doorknob. Your agent has a key to the box, as do cooperating agents and members of your local real estate trade organization (for example, a local Board of Realtors). If you agree to this system—and really, it helps make showings infinitely more convenient—insist on the most secure gadget available. For example, ask for a computerized lockbox that requires an access code to open.

The Show Goes on without You

Agents will likely show your house when you're not there. Normally, you will know in advance if a tour is scheduled. But on occasion an agent won't be able to contact you before a showing. Make sure that agents know that they must leave a business card in a conspicuous spot—the kitchen table, perhaps—before leaving your house after such a tour. Conversely, you will want to contact your own agent to let him or her know that the house has been shown. Your agent can then follow-up with the cooperating agent and buyers.

Once in a great while an agent will ring your doorbell and ask to show the house to a buyer who is waiting in the car. They were just driving by your house on the way to another showing, the salesperson will say, and they saw your For Sale sign. Ask for the agent's business card and, if at all possible, allow the agent and the buyer to see your house.

The Grand Tour

While you're certainly not going to stick around for the whole showing, you should try to be at home when your agent arrives with the prospects. Welcome the buyers and introduce yourself. Encourage them to spend all the time they need looking at your house. Give the agent any necessary instructions for locking up when he or she leaves. Then go out for your coffee.

As noted above, you might feel uncomfortable watching strangers tour your house. Your agent may want you to leave out of fear that, if you start to really chat with the prospects, you'll tip your negotiating hand. And there's a third reason to consider leaving the premises during the showing.

Buyers find it difficult to openly discuss what they like and dislike about a property when the owner is standing nearby. Competent salespeople can overcome a load of objections, but they can't read minds. They won't know what the buyers dislike if they fail to express themselves.

Here's an example. You've laid brown-and-yellow shag carpet in your family room. You think it has a cozy, homey feel. The buyers, however, hate it, but they don't tell you that. They don't want to offend. So you may have just lost a sale over $400 worth of carpeting.

If you've removed yourself from the situation, buyers will be much more inclined to express their dislikes. The buyers and your real estate agent can actually talk about the problem. The discussion might go something like this:

Buyer: Wow, that's ugly.

Agent: What's ugly?

Buyer: That brown-and-yellow shag.

Agent: You don't like the color?

Buyer: No.

Agent: What kind of carpet would your prefer?

Buyer: I like beige Berber. It goes with anything.

Agent: I see. You know, some beige Berber carpeting would really open up this room, wouldn't it?

Buyer: Sure would.

Agent: If the owners agree to change the carpet, would you be interested in owning this house?

Buyer: Yeah. The rest of the place is great, but I just can't live with that brown-and-yellow shag.

FSBO Showings

Of course, if you've taken the FSBO route, you have no choice but to stay in the house during showings. You're the one showing the house. We talked a bit about showing techniques in chapter 3. Now let's look at the situation in more detail.

You need to elicit the buyers' feelings about your property. This can be difficult. They won't want to hurt you, but you need to know what they dislike. Only after you've uncovered their problems with the house can you begin to overcome them. You don't want to lose a sale solely because the buyers hate the wallpaper in your bedroom. You'd rather repaper, and close the deal. Here's how you do it.

Greet the buyers when they enter the house and begin your tour. In general, you should invite them to look in all the cupboards and closets, try the faucets and the shower, flush the toilets, and try the heating and air-conditioning systems.

Give the buyers a little time to look around each room, then ask questions such as "How would your living room furniture look in this type of layout?" or "Will this carpet enhance the colors of your furniture?" Encourage the buyers to express their thoughts. State sincerely that you will not be offended by their comments. You are searching for ways to make simple changes as needed to satisfy the buyers' wishes. The more they talk, the more you get to know their needs, and the easier those needs become to satisfy.

Let's say you're touring the kitchen. Let your buyers explore the cupboards and closets, turn on the water, and try out the garbage disposal. Then ask, "Does this room have any features that your current kitchen doesn't?" If the buyers say, "Yeah. We've always wanted a garbage disposal," you say how much easier that appliance has made your life. Then ask if there would be anything the buyers would change about this room if they decided to purchase the place. If they say they'd like a different color paint, you might consider offering to repaint. If they say they'd like a new linoleum floor, you might consider laying a new linoleum floor.

Follow this pattern as you enter each of the rooms. Don't talk too much. Give the buyers a chance to look, to explore, and to discover. Point out features they might be likely to miss.

At the end of the tour, get each visitor's name, address, and phone number. Have them jot it down in your house book (discussed in chapter 3). Then follow up. Call the day after the showing to see if the buyers have any additional questions that you can answer. Then ask if they are interested in owning your house. (Say "own" not "buy." The former has much more positive connotations.) If the buyers hesitate, ask "What would it take for you to prepare an offer for my house today?" If they say, "New carpeting throughout," it might be worth it for you to install new wall-to-wall carpeting.

During your follow-up, ask the buyers how your house compares to others they have seen. It's good for you to know how you stack up against the competition. If several buyers find your property lacking, take their opinions to heart. You may be able to minimize any drawbacks. For example, if several buyers say, "I really like your house, but the noise from the street was driving me a little nuts," you may want to hire a

landscaper to plant mature shrubs around the perimeter of your property. Because these shrubs will buffer the noise, future buyers won't hear the rumble of the big rigs.

Nothing's Happening

You keep the place spotless. You show the property or make it convenient for agents to show it. Still, nothing. No offers. Not even a nibble.

What are you doing wrong? Quite possibly nothing. The length of time it takes to sell a house often depends on the economy—both locally and nationally. You have no control over this. Or maybe everybody else on the block chose this month to market their houses, too. Nothing you can do about that, either.

Or, of course, maybe no one's buying because you priced the house too high, didn't market it properly, or made it difficult for your agent to show the place.

Let's take a look at the issues that cause houses to remain on the market—both those you can do something about and those you can't.

- *Product.* Your house is your product. If the property isn't selling, you need to think of whether you have a nice product or a not-so-nice one. If it's the latter, consider what more you can do to spruce it uo. This situation is discussed more thoroughly later in this chapter.

- *Price.* If absolutely no one is making an offer, it's time to consider whether you've priced your house too high. (This is discussed extensively in chapter 6.)

- *Terms of sale.* The terms of sale include such items as the type of financing you'll allow, closing dates, and personal items (for example, the drapes or that washer-dryer combo) that you're willing to leave with the property. You can control the terms of sale and bend when necessary. For example, many sellers don't want to deal with buyers whose mortgages will be insured by the Federal Housing Administration (see chapter 8 for more information). If you've said "No FHA buyers," fine. But remember, such a decision may delay the sale of your house. If you're insisting that

today's lookers give you four months to close, fine. But if they need to move in within a month, you've lost a buyer.

- *Competition and market conditions.* You can't do anything about the 67 properties comparable to yours that now sit on the market. You can't, on your own, boost the national economy so that more people want to buy. You can, however, market your house in a way that separates it from the competition. Consider selling it at the lower end of its price range, offer a higher commission to real estate agents (they'll go where the money is), or offer to help would-be buyers with their closing costs. Get creative!

- *Marketing.* If you're a FSBO, sit down and reevaluate your ad campaign, using the techniques discussed in chapter 3. Are your ads attention grabbing? If not, consider rewriting or reproducing these spots. If you work with a real estate agent, sit down together to rethink the marketing plan for your house.

Reevaluating Your Position

Let's say your house has been on the market for several months. You've had a number of showings but no offers. That means that your marketing has proven effective; it's certainly getting people in the door. It also means that there are buyers out there qualified to purchase in your price range, so you can't blame the economy. So what's wrong?

Maybe you priced your house too high. Maybe you offered unfavorable terms. Or maybe your house just doesn't show well.

Go back and review the competition. You can do it with an agent or on your own, reviewing sale documents housed at the county courthouse. You need to ask the following questions:

- How many properties in your price range sit on the market right now?

- How many properties in that price range sat on the market when you first offered your house for sale?

- How many of these properties have sold in the last month?

- Where are they?

- What style are they (ranch, two story, etc.)?

- How large are they?

- How many bedrooms and bathrooms do they have?

- What amenities do they boast?

With this information in hand, you can begin to figure out how your house compares to similar properties in terms of product, price, and terms.

Look at your house as objectively as you can. Make sure the place is spotless. Consider whether there are any relatively inexpensive ways to make it look more expensive. If all it would take is a little elbow grease, get greasing. Or think about spending a few hundred bucks to replace your dingy carpeting with fresh, inexpensive, wall-to-wall carpeting. Get the exterior painted, if it needs it.

In chapter 6 we talked a lot about competitive pricing. If you're pricing your 3,000 square-foot home at $180,000, and all the other 3,000 square-foot houses are going for $162,000, you have priced yourself right out of the market. Consider coming down. Now.

"But," you may say, "I priced my house at $180,000, and all the other 3,000 square-foot houses are going for $180,000. What's wrong?"

Consider whether these houses boast amenities that yours doesn't. Buyers may be willing to pay extra for features such as finished basements, pools or saunas, and lovely landscaping. If your house offers none of these and all the comparably priced properties boast them all, you'll need to lower your price to compete.

Savvy homesellers know that buyers will often up their prices to get a break on the terms. And insisting on cash only or its equivalent (financing at the bank) might prove too limiting in your market at this time.

Some homesellers don't like to deal with buyers whose loans are insured by the Federal Housing Authority or the Veterans Administration. They know that these organizations often demand that certain repairs be made to a house before closing. Consider opening your doors to these customers. Hey, any buyer would have eventually demanded that you fix those rotting roof shingles.

Finally, if the silence of no phones ringing is deafening, it may be because you've got a bum marketing plan. Rethink it now. Don't just tout your house as the perfect place for young marrieds when it would serve retired empty nesters just as well. Don't only advertise your house to families with lots of kids when it may be the perfect spot for a mature couple that needs extra space for aging in-laws. Rethink your marketing strategies and shift them occasionally to appeal to a new audience. And be mindful of fair housing regulations in all of your advertisements. Excluding specific types of buyers, or even appealing explicitly to a certain category of buyer, is a violation of fair housing laws.

How quickly your house sells depends, to a large extent, on the price, product, marketing, and terms decision you make. Remain openminded and flexible, and one of these days you'll meet the right buyer.

Bottom-Line Thinking

By now, you should have a clue about:

- How long it takes to sell a house

- How to schedule showings

- How to show the property

- How to reevaluate your position if the place isn't moving

The Garage Sale

Sometime between putting your house on the market and closing on the property (and maybe *before* you put your house on the market if you want to clear stuff out to make the place roomier), you're going to want to get rid of a lot of your junk. The crib that your 15-year-old doesn't seem to need anymore; your batik clothes from the '60s—you get the gist.

You can bring in some nice garage sale bucks if you follow these tips:

- Place a classified ad in the local papers, including directions and other pertinent details. Take advantage of free publicity provided by bulletin boards in grocery stores and other public places.

- Merchandise your items attractively in neat, clean surroundings. Paper tablecloths offer a pretty setting for glass and ornamental items. Cluster things in categories; place the most desirable items in the back of the garage so browsers have no choice but to look at other merchandise on their way to the good stuff. Locate your appliance table near an outlet so customers may try before they buy.

- Add neighborhood signage—posted on telephone poles, buildings, or on the sidewalk. These signs are very effective.

- Keep plenty of paper bags and boxes on hand for packing breakable items.

- Keep plenty of one dollar bills and plenty of change on hand.

- Call a charitable organization to pick up any merchandise that remains after the conclusion of your sale.

THE Fish Are Biting

CHAPTER EIGHT

Just when you feel you can't scrub the kitchen floor once more, can't afford another ad, and can't stand one more showing, someone comes up with an offer. A choir of angels begins to sing The Hallelujah Chorus *in your head.*

But because you've never sold a house before, even the blessed offer can seem a chore. Packed with legal mumbo jumbo, it's hard to read. Worse, it may be written not only for several grand less than the price at which you marketed the property, but several grand less than the minimum you're willing to accept. Your agent or lawyer suggests you counteroffer, and you don't even know what that term means.

Read this chapter and you'll get a clue about:

- Understanding the offer

- When the offer becomes a binding contract

- Typical negotiable items

- Negotiating strategies

- Your rights and obligations under the contract

- How to handle multiple offers

- What to do if the sale falls through

An Offer or an Agreement?

When a buyer draws up an offer for your house, it does not legally bind you in any way until you sign it. At that point, this little piece of paper, listing all the terms of your sale, becomes a contract or a "purchase agreement."

To be valid, any contract must contain the following

- *Offer.* Someone offers to do something for someone else in exchange for some type of compensation. In this case, a buyer offers you money in exchange for your house.

- *Legally competent parties.* Anyone signing a purchase agreement must be legally competent to do so. For example, you can't hold a 17-year-old to a contract. A 17-year-old is not legally allowed to sign a contract because such a person has yet to reach the age of legal adulthood, 18 or 21, depending on the locality.

- *Consideration.* Consideration is something of value offered by one party to another under the terms of the contract. In your case, the buyer is offering you money for your house.

- *Legal purpose.* Two parties cannot enter into a binding contract to buy and sell heroine because the possession and sale of that drug is illegal in this country. However, the possession and sale of a house is eminently legal.

- *Adequate description.* The contract must describe your property. A street address, city, and state will usually do it.

- *In writing and signed by all parties.* The contract must be signed and in writing to be enforceable.

Offers: The Nitty-Gritty

In a bid, the buyer will offer to purchase your house at a certain price and under certain terms and conditions.

Ask your lawyer or agent for a sample purchase agreement when you put your house on the market. You want to understand all its provisions. Talk to your lawyer about any questions you may have. That way, you'll be better prepared to understand exactly what is being offered when your buyer writes up a bid for real.

Depending on your location, the agreement can run anywhere from one page to a veritable bundle. Read it and you'll find:

- The purchaser's name

- A description of the property, usually the street address, city, and state

- Your name

- Information on how the purchaser intends to take title

- How much the buyers are willing to pay for the property, and how they will pay for it. This includes information on mortgage financing and earnest and down payment amounts the buyers are willing to put up.

- The projected closing date

- A provision for obtaining a title search and insurance

- The method by which real estate taxes and other costs are to be prorated

- A provision for canceling the contract should the property be damaged or destroyed between the signing of the agreement and the closing date

- A liquidated damages clause, right-to-sue provision, or other statement of remedies available in the event of default. For example, liquidated damages is an amount of money predetermined by the buyer and the seller in a purchase agreement as the total compensation due to the injured party should the other party breach the agreement. A right-to-sue provision is a "contingency" (see below) or condition in a purchase agreement in which each party allows the other to sue for something greater than liquidated damages should a party breach the contract.

- Contingency clauses covering home inspections, the buyers obtaining financing, the buyers selling their current property, the sellers finding the home of their choice, and other issues. In general, contingency clauses cover additional conditions that the parties agree to over and above those in the contract (see "Residential Purchase Agreement" in Appendix A).

- An agency disclosure statement detailing who is representing whom (see chapter 4)

- A list of personal property to be left on the premises for the purchaser

- A list of property to be removed by the seller before the closing

- How to transfer any applicable warranties on items such a furnaces, air-conditioning units, or built-in appliances

- The identification of any leased equipment such as a water softener and whether it will be removed or transferred to the buyer

- Closing and settlement instructions regarding the transfer of any escrow funds; the transfer of payments for special assessments; the purchaser's right to a final walk-through before closing

To turn this offer into a binding contract, you need the dated signatures of each party.

Sample Contingencies

A *contingency* is a buyer's agreement to purchase your property only if certain conditions are met. Contingency clauses usually include a statement of necessary action, a timeline for their completion, and a notation of who will pay for what. Here's the wording of some common contingencies.

Purchasers Selling Their Own Property

Often your buyers will make their offer contingent on selling their own house. The contingency clause runs something like this:

> This offer is expressly subject to the Purchaser closing on the Purchaser's property located at 123 Main Street, Anytown, Any State, on or before _____ (fill in date). In the event that this condition is not met, this offer shall become null and void and the earnest money shall be refunded to the purchaser.

You learned in chapter 7 that you do not take your house off the market until the deal is done. So you keep marketing the place while the buyers work to sell their own house. But what if their place doesn't sell, and you start to get other offers?

Include an escape contingency of your own. It ought to run something like this:

> Due to the sale of home contingency in the Purchase Agreement, it is mutually agreed that the Seller may continue to offer the subject property for sale. In the event of another offer on the subject property, Seller shall immediately deliver to the Purchaser written notification of Seller's intent to accept said offer.

> The Purchaser shall have _____ (fill in number) hours from the time that Purchaser receives said notification to eliminate the sale of home contingency. Purchaser will provide written confirmation of ability to secure financing without such contingency, and be prepared to close within the dates set forth within the Agreement.

In the event Purchaser fails to eliminate said contingency within said
_____ (fill in number) hour period, this Agreement shall become null
and void and the earnest money shall be refunded to the Purchaser.

I'm a Buyer, You're a Buyer

You won't want to sell your current digs if you can't find another house to suit your
needs. A contingency covering this possibility might read:

This offer is expressly subject to the Sellers obtaining a firm commitment
for purchase of the home of their choice on or before _____
(fill in date). If this condition is not removed by the Sellers by
_____ (fill in date), this offer shall become null and void and
the earnest money shall be refunded to the Purchaser.

Negotiations

You've received and reviewed an offer but you don't like what the buyers have bid.
Maybe they offered too little money. Maybe they insist that you leave your above-
ground pool on the property. Or maybe they want to be in the house a week from
Tuesday and you aren't closing on your new place for a month.

What points can you negotiate? All of them! Here are some of the issues that will
probably most concern you:

- *Price.* Unless you are marketing a hot house in a hot market, your buyers
  will probably not meet your asking price in their first offer. You can
  either accept whatever price they proffer, reject it or, more commonly,
  counter their offer (counteroffer) with one of your own, bringing your
  price down slightly from the list price and up a bit from what the buyers
  initially suggested.

- *Financing.* You usually want the biggest down payment you can get, both
  for your own cash flow and as an assurance that the buyers are financially stable enough to qualify for a mortgage. (Contracting with preap-

proved buyers—or buyers whose bank has already OK'd them for a mortgage in your price range—can, of course, remove this concern from your mind.) And because you want a smooth sale, you made it clear in your listing agreement that you don't want any buyer who is planning on FHA-insured financing. This type of financing is usually preferred by buyers who don't have a lot to spend on a down payment. The FHA may require repairs on the house before it agrees to back the buyers' loan—and you'd rather avoid the red tape. However, depending on the number of offers you've received and your desire to get out of the house, you may want to consider dropping the amount of the down payment or earnest money required and start to think about FHA-insured buyers. If you really want to sell, you may even consider owner financing. (See sidebar.)

- *Closing and possession dates.* You may have said that you need to stay in your house until November 17th. But you have a buyer who's offering a good price on your house and needs to get in by October 30th. You might want to consider camping out in a hotel or with friends for a few weeks.

OWNER FINANCING

If you really, really need to sell, you might consider financing the deal yourself. This is called *owner financing*. This is how it usually works.

The buyer gives you an amount of money at closing for the down payment and makes regular monthly payments to you at an agreeable interest rate. These payments continue until the loan is paid off or until such date as the new owner is required to refinance.

You can draw buyers with owner financing, but you should only consider the deal if you're operating in a very strong buyer's market and if you don't immediately need too much cash from the sale of your house.

Negotiating Styles

Everything, you know, can be negotiated. But you don't know exactly how to start the process. Try adopting a win-win attitude. It works like this.

As the seller, you want to get a good price for your property. And you want the buyers to end up with a product that makes them happy.

You aim to strike a deal that both of you can live with. This type of attitude will affect all your discussion with the buyer. It will make you more reasonable and, therefore, help the negotiations proceed more smoothly.

This is a direct contrast to the "defeat" negotiation style—in which you try to win a battle against your buyer-opponent—and the "accommodating" negotiation style—in which you cave in to every buyer demand, regardless of whether those demands do your sale irreparable harm.

A seller who shouts, "This is my house. It's listed for $225,000 and I won't take a penny less," has embarked on a negative negotiating path.

A seller who says, "Oh, I see. You like my $225,000 house but you only have $175,000 to spend? Sure, I'll come down 50K," is perhaps too accommodating.

A creative homeseller who has adopted a win-win attitude might face the following type of situation:

The sellers have marketed their house at $210,000, and want to accept no less than $200,000. The buyers have offered $195,000. As part of the purchase agreement, the buyers have requested that they be able to take possession on June 15th, but the seller would rather stay in the property until June 30th. Additionally, the buyers have told the sellers that they are willing to let the sellers take the chandeliers that hang in the dining room and the foyer and the washer-dryer combo.

The sellers, trying to devise a deal that both parties can live with, call relatives to see if they can bunk with them for two weeks. The relatives say they'd love to have them. This frees up the sellers to offer the buyers the closing date they want—possibly saving them a grand or so in temporary housing costs. Then the sellers tell the buyers they can keep the chandeliers and the washer-dryer combo. In return for all this, the sellers ask that the buyers up their price to $200,000.

The buyers take a look at the counteroffer and agree to it. Everybody wins.

Who Has to Bend?

You've adopted a win-win attitude toward negotiations. Now, though, you may wonder which party gets to win a little more.

You're in a strong negotiating position if you operate in a seller's market or if you don't have a set time frame for moving out of the house; that is, if you don't have to sell. Also, buyers strongly motivated to move to your house—for a job transfer, for example—can buffer your position.

Buyers have the edge if there are more properties for sale than there are people shopping; if they have been preapproved for financing; and if they don't have a place to sell before they close on a new property.

Negotiating Strategy

Now that you've adopted a win-win attitude, it's time to plot your negotiating strategy. Keep your goal in mind: a deal that both you and the buyer can live with.

Don't hope for a sound negotiating strategy to simply materialize. You need to develop one with these steps in mind: prepare, discuss, bargain.

Prepare

In preparing for negotiations, you need to:

* *Define your objectives.* Determine what goals you must meet, in terms of price, closing dates, or financing. Then think of where you can bend to reach these goals. If price is paramount, you might be able to bend on financing terms or possession dates. If you can bend on neither price nor financing, you might consider moving out earlier than anticipated. This

allows the buyers to move in when they want, saving the cost of temporary housing. Also, you may choose to throw in whichever perks you can—draperies or the above-ground sauna out back, for example.

- *Learn what you can about the buyers.* Find out what the buyers really need. Do they need to move into your house quickly, perhaps because of a job transfer or similar situation? Are they absolutely unable to up the price offered? Remember, buyers are not required to share this information with you. But they may, if you and your agent can convince them that you want to develop a deal that will make you both as happy as possible. Once you learn the buyers' true needs, you can determine in what areas you can bend to meet them.

Discuss

Set up a meeting with the buyers or their representative. During this meeting:

- *Have the buyers and their agent present their initial position without interruption.*

- *Ask questions to clarify any issues that confuse you.*

- *Test the buyers' commitment to their initial position.* If the buyers demand that you leave the drapes, would they be willing to pay a little more for the house?

- *Ask the buyers to justify a lowball price.* The buyers should present a CMA, and you should have presented one of your own, along with an appraisal. This can often help bring buyers around if their first offer was deliberately low simply because they wanted to see what they could get away with.

- *Send signals that indicate your willingness to negotiate.* And look for similar signals on the buyers' part. These can include your saying, "Well, we understand that you'd prefer we repaint the living room. That's certainly something we can discuss." Conversely, the buyers might say, "Look, we know we asked you to repaint the living room, but let's not slow down the sale over this issue."

Bargain

To successfully bargain, you must:

- *Employ if-then statements.* If the buyers are willing to up their price, then you will leave the drapes in the house. If the buyers will push back the closing, allowing you to stay in the house until you close on your new place, then you can drop the price slightly.

- *Keep searching for negotiating points.* Renovations may be one. "If we were willing to complete the remodeling work in the basement, then would you be willing to come closer to our list price?"

Bargaining is the essence of negotiation. Both sides want their interests met. Your negotiating style and your objectivity will go a long way toward making it happen.

When You Should Counteroffer

If you choose not to accept the offer that has been presented to you exactly as written, you in essence reject it and come up with a new proposal of your own. This is called a *counteroffer.* Before you draw one up, remember this: Because you have rejected the buyers' original offer, they are no longer bound to its terms. You once held the acceptance/rejection card. With your counteroffer, that card now sits in the buyer's hand.

Make sure that you counter your buyer's offer only for substantive reasons. Don't risk losing a buyer over some frivolous change. You don't want your best buyer to take a hike because you absolutely refuse to spend two hours repainting the bathroom.

Ditto with money issues. If you want $170,000 from the sale of your house, don't counter an offer of $168,500.

When presenting buyers with a counteroffer, give them a period of time in which to accept it, reject it, or come up with another offer of their own.

CALIFORNIA
ASSOCIATION
OF REALTORS®

COUNTER OFFER No. _____
(For use by Seller or Buyer. May be used for Multiple Counter.)

This is a counter offer to the: ☐ Offer, ☐ Counter Offer, ☐ Other _____, dated _____,
regarding (property address): _____
between _____, "Buyer," and _____, "Seller."

1. **TERMS:** The terms and conditions of the above referenced document are accepted subject to the following:
   A. Paragraphs in the purchase contract (offer) which require initials by all parties, but are not initialed by all parties, are excluded from the final agreement unless specifically referenced for inclusion in paragraph 1C of this or another Counter Offer.
   B. Unless otherwise specified in writing, down payment and loan amount(s) will be adjusted in the same proportion as in the original offer.
   C. _____
   _____
   _____
   _____
   _____
   _____
   _____
   _____
   _____
   _____
   _____
   _____
   _____
   _____
   _____
   _____
   _____
   _____
   _____
   _____
   _____

   D. The following attached supplements are incorporated in this Counter Offer:
   ☐ _____   ☐ _____
   ☐ _____   ☐ _____

2. ☐ **(If Checked:) MULTIPLE COUNTER OFFER:** Seller is making a Counter Offer(s) to another prospective buyer(s) on terms which may or may not be the same as in this Counter Offer. Acceptance of this Counter Offer by Buyer shall **not** be binding unless and until it is subsequently re-signed by Seller in paragraph 7 below. Prior to the completion of all of these events, Buyer and Seller shall have no duties or obligations for the purchase or sale of the Property.

3. **RIGHT TO ACCEPT OTHER OFFERS:** Seller reserves the right to continue to offer the Property for sale or for other transaction, and to accept any other offer at any time prior to communication of acceptance, as described in paragraph 4. Seller's acceptance of another offer prior to Buyer's acceptance and communication of acceptance of this Counter Offer shall revoke this Counter Offer.

4. **EXPIRATION:** Unless acceptance of this Counter Offer is signed by the person receiving it, and communication of acceptance is made by delivering a signed copy in person, by mail, or by facsimile which is personally received, to the person making this Counter Offer or to _____, by 5:00 PM on the third calendar day after this Counter Offer is written (or, if checked, ☐ date: _____, time _____ AM/PM), this Counter Offer shall be deemed revoked and the deposit shall be returned to Buyer. This Counter Offer may be executed in counterparts.

As the person(s) making this Counter Offer on the terms above, receipt of a copy is acknowledged.

_____ Date: _____ Time: _____ AM/PM

Date: _____ Time: _____ AM/PM

5. **ACCEPTANCE: I/WE** accept the above Counter Offer (If checked: ☐ **SUBJECT TO THE ATTACHED COUNTER OFFER**) and acknowledge receipt of a copy.

_____ Date: _____ Time: _____ AM/PM

_____ Date: _____ Time: _____ AM/PM

6. **ACKNOWLEDGMENT OF RECEIPT:** Receipt of signed acceptance on (date) _____, at _____ AM/PM, by the maker of the Counter Offer, or other person designated in paragraph 4, is acknowledged. (_____/_____) (Initials)

7. **MULTIPLE COUNTER OFFER SIGNATURE LINE: (Paragraph 7 applies only if paragraph 2 is checked.)** By signing below, Seller accepts this Multiple Counter Offer, and creates a binding contract. (NOTE TO SELLER: Do NOT sign in this paragraph until after Buyer signs the acceptance in paragraph 5, and returns to Seller for re-signing.)

_____ Date: _____ Time: _____ AM/PM

_____ Date: _____ Time: _____ AM/PM

THIS FORM HAS BEEN APPROVED BY THE CALIFORNIA ASSOCIATION OF REALTORS® (C.A.R.). NO REPRESENTATION IS MADE AS TO THE LEGAL VALIDITY OR ADEQUACY OF ANY PROVISION IN ANY SPECIFIC TRANSACTION. A REAL ESTATE BROKER IS THE PERSON QUALIFIED TO ADVISE ON REAL ESTATE TRANSACTIONS. IF YOU DESIRE LEGAL OR TAX ADVICE, CONSULT AN APPROPRIATE PROFESSIONAL.

This form is available for use by the entire real estate industry. It is not intended to identify the user as a REALTOR®. REALTOR® is a registered collective membership mark which may be used only by members of the NATIONAL ASSOCIATION OF REALTORS® who subscribe to its Code of Ethics.

The copyright laws of the United States (17 U.S. Code) forbid the unauthorized reproduction of this form by any means, including facsimile or computerized formats.
Copyright © 1986-1997, CALIFORNIA ASSOCIATION OF REALTORS®

Published and Distributed by:
REAL ESTATE BUSINESS SERVICES, INC.
a subsidiary of the CALIFORNIA ASSOCIATION OF REALTORS®
525 South Virgil Avenue, Los Angeles, California 90020   Page _____ of _____ Pages.

OFFICE USE ONLY
Reviewed by Broker
or Designee _____
Date _____

COUNTER OFFER (CO-14 PAGE 1 OF 1) REVISED 9/95

Reprinted with permission, California Association of REALTORS®. Endorsement not implied.

If the buyer fails to respond to your offer in the time allotted, withdraw it in writing. Otherwise, the buyer may accept your counter at the same time you are selling your house to someone else. You have, in essence, sold the same house twice. You don't want that.

Considering Multiple Offers

If you're operating in a great seller's market, you may find yourself in the enviable position of having to simultaneously consider a number of offers.

Schedule appointments to meet each buyer. Chat with each separately. Don't bargain with anyone until you have determined which is your best offer. Invite your best buyer in for another meeting, and begin the bargaining process. If you can't reach an agreement, call your second-best buyer back in.

You might choose to accept one offer as the primary offer and a second one as a back-up, to be used if the first falls through for any reason.

Signing the Contract

A signed purchase agreement affords certain rights to both seller and buyer and mandates they each assume certain responsibilities, as outlined below.

Sellers have the right to:

- Accept an offer from any buyer.

- Reject an offer from anyone they choose not to sell to, as long as the decision not to sell doesn't violate fair housing requirements (see chapter 4).

- Counter any offers proffered.

Sellers are obligated to:

- Sign a Property Condition Disclosure Form. Owners of homes built before 1978 must also sign a Lead-Based Paint Disclosure Form (see chapter 4).

- Honor the terms of any offers accepted.

- Deliver a title to the property that is free and clear of all liens and encumbrances (discussed thoroughly in chapter 9).

- Stand behind their promise that any heating, air-conditioning, plumbing, and heating systems were left in working order at the time of the sale.

- Leave any fixtures and personal property in the house as agreed with the buyers.

- Allow the buyer to conduct any inspections agreed to in the purchase agreement.

- Allow the buyer to enter your house for a final walk-through.

- Pay any applicable commissions.

- Pay the existing insurance on the house until the closing of the transaction.

Those are your rights and obligations as the seller. Now let's take a look at the buyer's rights and obligations.

Buyers have a right to:

- Offer to purchase your house at whatever price they choose.

- Choose their own financing.

- Offer whatever earnest money or down payment they choose.

- Request that certain personal property (draperies, window air-conditioning units, etc.) be included in the sale.

- Ask you to pay part of their closing costs.

- Demand that you pay property taxes until the date of closing.

Paying the Broker
if You Default

If your sale falls through because you have defaulted on any terms of the purchase agreement, you probably still have to pay your broker a commission. Say, for example, you agree to close on the house on January 17th. Then, for whatever reason, you change your mind, saying, "I'll be damned if I'll get out of here before the end of February." Because of this, your buyer backs out of the transaction. You probably still owe the broker a commission if that broker has fulfilled his or her obligations per your listing agreement.

You can also be required to write your broker a check if you refuse an offer that meets your list price and conditions of sale.

Disputes over the broker's commission in cases such as these are often settled in arbitration or in a court of law, where a third-party judge makes the final determination based on the facts and in accordance with all of the written agreements between the parties.

- Expect that heating, air-conditioning , plumbing, and electrical systems are left in working order.

- Have the house inspected at their expense.

- Take a final tour, or walk-through, of your house shortly before closing.

- Purchase additional home insurance on the property if they feel that you are not adequately covered.

- Retain a lawyer to examine your title.

Buyers are obligated to:

- Fulfill the terms and conditions of the purchase agreement.

- Have their agreed-upon earnest money available for deposit in an escrow account.

- Forfeit their earnest money if they default on the agreement.

- Allow you to take any personal property with you when you move, as long as that property was not listed in the purchase agreement.

What to Do if the Sale Falls Through

The buyer's transfer fell through. He couldn't get financing. Aunt Matilda unexpectedly decided against lending him the money for the down payment. He got fired. Whatever.

All that matters to you is your deal fell through. What to do?

Start again. Agents should redouble their marketing efforts on your behalf. FSBOs should recontact anyone who has shown interest in the place, to let them know it is back on the market.

It's a depressing and tough row to hoe, but you have no choice. And take heart. You already found one buyer who loved the place. You'll find another.

Bottom-Line Thinking

By now, you should have a clue about:

- The difference between an offer and a purchase agreement

- How to prepare for negotiations with potential buyers

- Adopting a win-win attitude while bargaining

- Points of negotiation

- How to consider multiple offers

- Your rights and responsibilities, and the buyer's rights and responsibilities

ON Your WAY?

CHAPTER NINE

You've accepted an offer. Terrific! Now you only have to wade through the paperwork of closing. If you've chosen to work with a real estate agent, you have a guide through the process. If not, you may have to guide yourself.

Read this chapter and you'll get a clue about:

- What lenders will require from you

- What title and closing companies will require from you

- What insurance companies and appraisers will want from you

- What to do the day of the closing

- How to coordinate your move

Before Closing

Just because you've received an offer doesn't necessarily mean that you can twiddle your thumbs until closing day. Both you and the buyer have things to do, and things to buy. The number of chores already completed by you and the buyer determines how quickly you can close. It may be only a few weeks. Unfortunately, though, the waiting period—especially when dealing with a buyer who was not preapproved for a mortgage on your property—can take a month or more.

Here's a chronological list of what needs to be done.

THE CLOSING STATEMENT

Your closing agent will prepare a closing statement for you, showing your closing credits (what you make from the sale of the house) and your closing debits (the amount left on your current mortgage that you have to pay off plus any closing costs you have assumed).

This statement will be updated regularly, with a final copy mailed to you a few days before closing.

You Have to Contact Your Closing Officer

After you've accepted an offer, your closing officer will take hold of the purchase agreement and any earnest money offered by the buyers.

Once the buyer has secured financing, the closing officer will start putting together the closing paperwork. You and the buyer will receive a preliminary report, indicating whether anyone other than you has a legal claim to the property. For example, if you have failed to pay your property taxes, your municipality may have slapped a lien on the house. Any buyer will demand that you pay off this lien before closing.

The closing officer will also contact you to give you "payoff" information from lenders to whom you currently owe mortgage money.

The Buyer Has to Meet Lender Requirements

If you followed the advice offered earlier in this book, you probably went with a buyer who was preapproved for financing a house in your price range. Unless the buyer goes on a spending binge and his or her finances are reevaluated unfavorably, only an appraisal and possibly a home inspection stands between you and the close. The time from offer to close may run only a week or two.

If you accepted an offer from a buyer who has yet to get a financing commitment, you'll have to wait considerably longer. The buyer needs time to select a lender, undergo a credit check, and wait while the institution verifies employment, income, and so forth. During this time, either you or your agent should stay in close touch with the buyer to learn whether the mortgage application is proceeding smoothly.

The House Must Be Inspected

You may have had this service performed already. If not, now's the time.

The House Must Be Appraised

The lender typically reviews two things before granting a loan: the creditworthiness of the borrower and the marketability of the property. The lender will demand an appraisal to prove that the house is worth the money it's lending the buyers.

The greater the down payment the buyers offer, the more lenient the appraisal will be. Often, the lower the down payment the more financially unstable the buyer. Therefore, the property must be more critically appraised to assure resale value if the buyer defaults.

As discussed earlier in this book, it's best for you to have the house appraised before putting it on the market. If you have not, someone—either you or the buyer—will certainly have to foot the bill for this service before closing. (If the buyer is applying for a mortgage, the appraisal will be required as part of the mortgage application; in which case, the buyer pays for sure.)

You Have to Prepare for Your Move

Your new buyers will likely want you outta there the moment you close, so chances are your actual moving chores need to be completed before you sign over the deed to your old house. Moving tips are addressed later in this chapter.

You Must Perform a Title Search and Purchase Title Insurance

Most lenders will demand a title search to ensure that no one else but you holds any right to your property. During the search, professionals from abstract companies or title companies will peruse public records to make sure that you really own the house and have the sole right to sell it. The seller customarily pays for this service, and the buyer usually pays for title insurance.

You may wonder why, if you're paying for a search, you have to pay for insurance.

Easy. The people who researched your title no doubt did their best. But, on occasion, a title claim is so convoluted, or sits so far in the past, that they miss it. You didn't know that one of the home's previous owners left, in her will, an 8 percent share of it to her favorite great niece. No one needs the great niece showing up, demanding a piece of the action. Title insurance protects the lender against such an eventuality. So, sellers customarily pay this fee, as well.

The Buyer Must Purchase Homeowners Insurance

The buyer's lender will probably demand proof of homeowners insurance. This is always paid by the buyer. It generally insures the homeowner against the following:

- Fire and lightning

- Glass breakage

- Windstorm and hail

- Explosion

- Riots

- Damage by aircraft

- Damage from car wrecks

- Smoke damage

- Vandalism

- Theft

The Buyer Will Take a Final Tour of the Property

If your buyers have done their homework, they will insist on touring the house one more time before closing. In real estate parlance this is known as the final "walk-through." (See checklist on page 128.) The buyers want to ensure that you're leaving the place in the same condition in which they bought it. They'll also make a last-minute check of all heating, cooling, and plumbing systems. Finally, they'll make sure that any goods they are paying for are still in the house—the sauna, the washing machine, and the dishwasher, for example.

The Closing

Closing is simply the procedure through which you relinquish any claim to the property and new owners take possession. You hand over the title; the buyers hand over the bucks.

Different states and communities handle closings differently. In some areas, custom mandates that the closing be held in the listing seller's brokerage firm. In other areas a lawyer (the buyer's or seller's) handles it. In still other areas, the buyer's lender, escrow company, or title company will rule the show. Your agent or lawyer can tell you what customs prevail in your city.

Walk-Through Checklist

Date of Inspection: _____

Address: _____

Approved

Appliances: (if warranted)
    Start dishwasher and run through cycle   _____
    Check ice in refrigerator   _____
    Turn on garbage disposal   _____
    Turn on fan and light in hood   _____
    Turn on trash compactor   _____

Plumbing:
    Run all faucets and check for leaks   _____
    Check under sinks for leaks   _____
    Turn on all showers   _____
    Put water in tubs to check drains   _____

Electric:
    Turn on ceiling fans   _____
    Check rheostat switches   _____
    Turn on exhaust fans in bathrooms   _____
    Check doorbell   _____
    Check intercom system   _____
    Check garage door openers   _____
    Check sump pump   _____

Make sure all blinds or draperies are in working order   _____
Check furnace/air conditioner   _____
Make sure doors close and latch properly   _____
Make sure windows close and lock   _____
Be sure that all items that are to stay are still in the house   _____
Check all items that are a part of the offer   _____

Other:_____

_____

_____

Who Should Attend the Closing?

The closing is like a huge "we sold the house party," except without the food, fun, and beer. You'll run into a number of people. Depending on which customs prevail in your area, and who hired agents to represent their interests, you'll probably encounter the following people:

- The buyer

- The buyer's lawyer

- Your lawyer

- The buyer's broker

- Your agent

- A representative from the buyer's lending institution

- A lawyer from the lending institution

- A representative from the title insurance company

What Do You Do at Closing?

The short answer is, you sign stuff and get your check.

You will have to sign deeds, title forms, and other documents. Your lawyer or agent will guide you through the process. You'll review the settlement statement to make sure the final figures are accurate.

You must also remember to give the buyers any keys to the house. These include house keys and mail box keys. You must turn over your garage door opener, and give the new owners the combination to any alarm system you have.

Coordinating the Move

In all the excitement of selling, don't forget to plan for moving.

If you move yourself you can get information from truck rental agencies to estimate the size of vehicle you will need. If you prefer to hire a professional moving company, ask for an estimate of the cost first. Then you can decide if you want them to do your packing or if you prefer to do it yourself. You can also decide whether you want to buy the boxes and cartons or if you want to begin stocking up on these items by asking local grocery and liquor stores to give you their throwaways.

There are all kinds of costs associated with a professional move, so be sure to interview and collect estimates from more than one reputable company. If one moving company's estimate is incredibly far afield from the others, you know something's wrong with it.

Because you've probably sold your old house to buy a new one, try to coordinate your two closings. The closing on your current house will typically take place first so that you have the funds available to buy your new place. Beware, though: while in some areas funds are disbursed at the closing table, people living in other locales have to wait up to a week for their money.

Now it's time to get packin'! Here are some tips:

- Don't load more than 50 pounds into any one box, and make sure the weight is evenly distributed. Cushion contents with newspaper or other packing material to prevent breakage.

- Pack all breakables and liquids separately. Seal medicines and other liquids to prevent leaking and pack them in an air-tight bag or container.

- Carry all of your valuables with you Don't pack into a van jewelry, documents, or anything else you can't replace—things such as great grandma's photo album or the Christmas ornaments your family has collected for decades.

DON'T FORGET THE UTILITIES

Prior to the closing, contact your utility company and get a final reading of gas, water, and electric meters. Coordinate the utility transfer with the companies in charge and with the buyers so that they enjoy uninterrupted services. And don't forget to coordinate with your sellers so that you enjoy uninterrupted service in your new digs.

- Have each family member pack an overnight suitcase so that if you arrive at your destination late, everyone will have important bedtime items. Also include a change of clothes for the next day.

Alerting Your Friends

Don't forget to take a few minutes off from your packing chores to send out change-of-address cards. You can pick them up at your local post office. Mail them off to the following:

- Family

- Friends

- Club members

- Doctors

- Insurance companies

- Your attorney

- Your accountant

- Charge card companies

- The magazines to which you subscribe

- Coworkers

- Anyone else with whom you correspond

It's a Wrap!

Selling your house is no mean feat. The entire process—from marketing the place to closing a transaction—entails so much work and, often, so many frustrations, that there are plenty of reasons not to move (see chapter 1).

But if you've read this far, you've likely decided to go for it. Good for you. Often, family conditions, business opportunities, or shrinking finances require that you sell. Sometimes you may just want a change of scene—and if you're in a sound seller's market, there's no reason in the world not to put your current digs on the block and go for your dream home. You've read this book, and by now you have a clue about:

- Determining whether you *need* to move or just *want* to move

- How to choose the right real estate agent

- How to sell your house on your own

- Laws governing real estate transactions

- How to determine the tax bite on the sale

- Preparing your house for showings

- Marketing strategies

- Pricing your house to sell

- Negotiating offers

- Closing the deal

Think of the hassle of selling your current abode as a rainbow. At the end, you'll find your pot of gold—a.k.a. a home that better suits your lifestyle. Your new place will be chock full of wonderful memories just waiting to happen.

Good luck with it.

APPENDIX

A

Residential Purchase Agreement

CALIFORNIA ASSOCIATION OF REALTORS®

RESIDENTIAL PURCHASE AGREEMENT
(AND RECEIPT FOR DEPOSIT)
For Use With Single Family Residential Property — Attached or Detached

Date: _____, at _____, California,

Received From _____ ("Buyer"),

A Deposit Of _____ Dollars $ _____, toward the

Purchase Price Of _____ Dollars $ _____,

For Purchase Of Property Situated In _____, County Of _____,

California, Described As _____, ("Property").

1. **FINANCING:** Obtaining the loans below **is a contingency** of this Agreement. Buyer shall act diligently and in good faith to obtain the designated loans. Obtaining deposit, down payment and closing costs **is not a contingency.**

    A. **BUYER'S DEPOSIT** shall be held uncashed until Acceptance and then deposited within 3 business days after . . $ _____
       Acceptance or ☐ _____ ☐ with Escrow Holder,
       ☐ into Broker's trust account, or ☐ _____, by ☐ Personal Check, ☐ Cashier's Check,
       ☐ Cash, or ☐ _____

    B. **INCREASED DEPOSIT** shall be deposited with _____ . . $ _____
       within _____ **Days** After Acceptance, or ☐ _____

    C. **FIRST LOAN IN THE AMOUNT OF** . . . . $ _____
       NEW First Deed of Trust in favor of LENDER, encumbering the Property, securing a note payable at maximum
       interest of _____ % fixed rate, or _____ % initial adjustable rate with a maximum interest rate cap of
       _____ %, balance due in _____ years. Buyer shall pay loan fees/points not to exceed _____.
          ☐ FHA ☐ VA: Seller shall pay (i) _____ % discount points, (ii) other fees not allowed to be paid by Buyer,
          not to exceed $ _____, and (iii) the cost of lender required repairs not otherwise provided for in
          this Agreement, not to exceed $ _____.

    D. **ADDITIONAL FINANCING TERMS:** _____ . . $ _____
       _____
       ☐ seller financing, (C.A.R. Form SFA-14); ☐ junior or assumed financing, (C.A.R. Form PAA-14, paragraph 5)

    E. **BALANCE OF PURCHASE PRICE** (not including costs of obtaining loans and other closing costs) to be deposited . . $ _____
       with escrow holder within sufficient time to close escrow.

    F. **TOTAL PURCHASE PRICE** . . . . $ _____

    G. **LOAN CONTINGENCY** shall remain in effect until the designated loans are funded (**or** ☐ _____ **Days** After Acceptance, by which time Buyer shall give Seller written notice of Buyer's election to cancel this Agreement if Buyer is unable to obtain the designated loans. If Buyer does not give Seller such notice, the contingency of obtaining the designated loans shall be removed by the method specified in paragraph 16B.)

    H. **LOAN APPLICATIONS; PREQUALIFICATION: For NEW financing,** within 5 (or ☐ _____) **Days** After Acceptance, Buyer shall provide Seller a letter from lender or mortgage loan broker stating that, based on a review of Buyer's written application and credit report, Buyer is prequalified for the NEW loan indicated above. If Buyer fails to provide such letter within that time, Seller may cancel this Agreement in writing.

    I. ☐ **APPRAISAL CONTINGENCY:** (If checked) This Agreement is contingent upon Property appraising at no less than the specified total purchase price. If there is a loan contingency, the appraisal contingency shall remain in effect until the loan contingency is removed, otherwise, the appraisal contingency shall be removed within 10 (or ☐ _____) **Days** After Acceptance.

    J. **ALL CASH OFFER:** If this is an all cash offer, Buyer shall, within 5 (or ☐ _____) **Days** After Acceptance, provide Seller written verification of sufficient funds to close this transaction. Seller may cancel this Agreement in writing within **5 Days** After: **(I)** time to provide verification expires, if Buyer fails to provide verification; or **(II)** receipt of verification, if Seller reasonably disapproves it.

2. **ESCROW:** Close Of Escrow shall occur _____ **Days** After Acceptance (or ☐ on _____ (date)). Buyer and Seller shall deliver signed escrow instructions consistent with this Agreement ☐ within _____ **Days** After Acceptance, ☐ at least _____ **Days** before Close Of Escrow, or ☐ _____. Seller shall deliver possession and occupancy of the Property to Buyer at _____ AM/PM, ☐ on the date of Close Of Escrow, ☐ no later than _____ **Days** After date of Close Of Escrow, **or** ☐ _____ _____. Property shall be vacant, unless otherwise agreed in writing. If transfer of title and possession do not occur at the same time, Buyer and Seller are advised to (a) consult with their insurance advisors, and (b) enter into a written occupancy agreement. The omission from escrow instructions of any provision in this Agreement shall not constitute a waiver of that provision.

3. **OCCUPANCY:** Buyer ☐ does, ☐ does not, intend to occupy Property as Buyer's primary residence.
4. **ALLOCATION OF COSTS:** (Check boxes which apply. If needed, insert additional instructions in blank lines.)
   GOVERNMENTAL TRANSFER FEES:
   A. ☐ Buyer ☐ Seller shall pay County transfer tax or transfer fee. _____
   B. ☐ Buyer ☐ Seller shall pay City transfer tax or transfer fee. _____
   TITLE AND ESCROW COSTS:
   C. ☐ Buyer ☐ Seller shall pay for **owner's** title insurance policy, issued by _____ company.
   (Buyer shall pay for any title insurance policy insuring Buyer's **Lender**, unless otherwise agreed.)
   D. ☐ Buyer ☐ Seller shall pay escrow fee. _____ Escrow holder shall be _____
   SEWER/SEPTIC/WELL COSTS:
   E. ☐ Buyer ☐ Seller shall pay for sewer connection, if required by Law prior to Close Of Escrow. _____
   F. ☐ Buyer ☐ Seller shall pay to have septic or private sewage disposal system inspected. _____
   G. ☐ Buyer ☐ Seller shall pay to have wells tested for water quality, potability, productivity, and recovery rate. _____
   OTHER COSTS:
   H. ☐ Buyer ☐ Seller shall pay Homeowners' Association transfer fees. _____
   I. ☐ Buyer ☐ Seller shall pay Homeowners' Association document preparation fees. _____
   J. ☐ Buyer ☐ Seller shall pay for zone disclosure reports. _____
   K. ☐ Buyer ☐ Seller shall pay for Smoke Detector installation and/or Water Heater bracing. _____
   Seller, prior to close of escrow, shall provide Buyer a written statement of compliance in accordance with state and local Law, unless exempt.
   L. ☐ Buyer ☐ Seller shall pay the cost of compliance with any other minimum mandatory government retrofit standards and inspections required
   as a condition of closing escrow under any Law. _____
   M. ☐ Buyer ☐ Seller shall pay the cost of a one year home warranty plan, issued by _____,
   with the following optional coverage _____. Policy cost not to exceed $ _____.
   PEST CONTROL REPORT:
   N. ☐ Buyer ☐ Seller shall pay for the Pest Control Report ("Report"), which, within the time specified in paragraph 16, shall be prepared by
   _____, a registered structural pest control company. _____
   O. (1) Buyer shall have the right to disapprove the Report as specified in paragraph 16, UNLESS any box in 4 O (2) is checked below
   OR (2) (Applies if any box is checked below)
   (a) ☐ Buyer ☐ Seller shall pay for work recommended to correct conditions described in the Report as **"Section 1."**
   (b) ☐ Buyer ☐ Seller shall pay for work recommended to correct conditions described in the Report as **"Section 2,"** unless waived by Buyer

   Buyer and Seller acknowledge receipt of copy of this page, which constitutes Page 1 of _____ Pages.

   Buyer's Initials (_____) (_____)   Seller's Initials (_____) (_____)

Published and Distributed by:
REAL ESTATE BUSINESS SERVICES, INC.
a subsidiary of the *CALIFORNIA ASSOCIATION OF REALTORS®*
525 South Virgil Avenue, Los Angeles, California 90020

REVISED 4/98

OFFICE USE ONLY
Reviewed by Broker
or Designee _____
Date _____

EQUAL HOUSING OPPORTUNITY

PRINT DATE

RESIDENTIAL PURCHASE AGREEMENT AND RECEIPT FOR DEPOSIT (RPA-14 PAGE 1 OF 5)

Property Address: _____ Date: _____

5.   **PEST CONTROL TERMS:** If a Report is prepared pursuant to paragraph 4N:
    A. The Report shall cover the main building and attached structures and, if checked: ☐ detached garages and carports, ☐ detached decks,
    ☐ the following other structures on the Property: _____.
    B. If Property is a unit in a condominium, planned development, or residential stock cooperative, the Report shall cover only the separate interest
    and any exclusive-use areas being transferred, and shall not cover common areas, unless otherwise agreed.
    C. If inspection of inaccessible areas is recommended in the Report, Buyer has the option, within 5 Days After receipt of the Report, either to accept
    and approve the Report by the method specified in paragraph 16B, or to request in writing that further inspection be made. If upon further
    inspection no infestation or infection is found in the inaccessible areas, the cost of the inspection, entry, and closing of those areas shall be paid
    for by Buyer. If upon further inspection infestation or infection is found in the inaccessible areas, the cost of inspection, entry, and closing of those
    areas shall be paid for by the party so designated in paragraph 4O(2)a. If no party is so designated, then cost shall be paid by Buyer.
    D. If no infestation or infection by wood destroying pests or organisms is found in the Report, or upon completion of required corrective work,
    a written Pest Control Certification shall be issued. Certification shall be issued prior to Close Of Escrow, unless otherwise agreed in writing.
    E. Inspections, corrective work and Pest Control Certification in this paragraph refers only to the presence or absence of wood destroying pests or
    organisms, and does not include the condition of roof coverings. Read paragraphs 9 and 12 concerning roof coverings.
    F. Nothing in paragraph 5 shall relieve Seller of the obligation to repair or replace shower parts and shower enclosures due to leaks, if required
    by paragraph 9B(3). Water test of shower pans on upper level units may not be performed unless the owners of property below the shower consent.

6.   **TRANSFER DISCLOSURE STATEMENT; NATURAL HAZARD DISCLOSURES;SUBSEQUENT DISCLOSURES; MELLO-ROOS NOTICE:**
    A. Within the time specified in paragraph 16A(1), if required by law, a Real Estate Transfer Disclosure Statement ("TDS") and Natural Hazard
    Disclosure Statement ("NHD") (or substituted disclosure) shall be completed and delivered to Buyer, who shall return signed copies to Seller.
    B. In the event Seller, prior to Close Of Escrow, becomes aware of adverse conditions materially affecting the Property, or any material inaccuracy
    in disclosures, information, or representations previously provided to Buyer (including those made in a TDS) of which Buyer is otherwise
    unaware, Seller shall promptly provide a subsequent or amended disclosure, in writing, covering those items, **except for those conditions and**
    material inaccuracies disclosed in reports obtained by Buyer.
    C. Seller shall (i) make a good faith effort to obtain a disclosure notice from any local agencies which levy a special tax on the Property pursuant
    to the Mello-Roos Community Facilities Act; and (ii) promptly deliver to Buyer any such notice made available by those agencies.
    D. If the TDS, the NHD (or substituted disclosure), the Mello-Roos disclosure notice, or a subsequent or amended disclosure is delivered to Buyer
    after the offer is signed, Buyer shall have the right to terminate this Agreement within **3 days** after delivery in person, or **5 days** after delivery by
    deposit in the mail, by giving written notice of termination to Seller or Seller's agent.

7.   **DISCLOSURES:** Within the time specified in paragraph 16A(1), Seller, shall (i) if required by law, disclose if Property is located in any zone identified
    in 7A; (ii) if required by law, provide Buyer with the disclosures and other information identified in 7B, and, (iii) if applicable, take the actions specified
    in 7C. Buyer shall then, within the time specified in paragraph 16, investigate the disclosures and information, and other information provided to
    Buyer, and provide written notice to Seller of any item disapproved.
    A. ZONE DISCLOSURES: Special Flood Hazard Areas; Potential Flooding (Inundation) Areas; Very High Fire Hazard Zones; State Fire
    Responsibility Areas; Earthquake Fault Zones; Seismic Hazard Zones; or any other federal, state, or locally designated zone for which disclosure
    is required by Law.
    B. **PROPERTY DISCLOSURES AND PUBLICATIONS:** Lead-Based Paint Disclosures and pamphlet; Earthquake Guides (and disclosures),
    Environmental Hazards Booklet, and Energy Efficiency Booklet (when published).
    C. ☐ (If checked:) **CONDOMINIUM/COMMON INTEREST SUBDIVISION:** Property is a unit in a condominium, planned development, or other
    common interest subdivision. Seller shall request from the Homeowners' Association ("HOA"), and upon receipt provide to Buyer: copies of
    covenants, conditions, and restrictions; articles of incorporation, by-laws, and other governing documents; statement regarding limited
    enforceability of age restrictions, if applicable; copies of most current financial documents distributed; statement indicating current regular,
    special and emergency dues and assessments, any unpaid assessment, any additional amounts due from Seller or Property, any approved
    changes to regular, special or emergency dues or assessments; preliminary list of defects, if any; any written notice of settlement regarding
    common area defects; and any pending or anticipated claims or litigation by or against the HOA; any other documents required by Law; a
    statement containing the location and number of designated parking and storage spaces; and copies of the most recent 12 months of HOA
    minutes for regular and special meetings, if available.
    D. **NOTICE OF VIOLATION:** If, prior to Close Of Escrow, Seller receives notice or is made aware of any notice filed or issued against the Property,
    for violations of any Laws, Seller shall immediately notify Buyer in writing.

8. TITLE AND VESTING:

A. Within the time specified in paragraph 16A, Buyer shall be provided a current preliminary (title) report (which is only an offer by the title insurer to issue a policy of title insurance, and may not contain every item affecting title). Buyer shall, within the time specified in paragraph 16A(2), provide written notice to Seller of any items reasonably disapproved.

B. At Close Of Escrow, Buyer shall receive a grant deed conveying title (or, for stock cooperative or long-term lease, an assignment of stock certificate or of seller's interest), including oil, mineral and water rights, if currently owned by Seller. Title shall be subject to all encumbrances, easements, covenants, conditions, restrictions, rights, and other matters which are of record or disclosed to Buyer prior to Close Of Escrow, unless disapproved in writing by Buyer within the time specified in paragraph 16A(2). However, title shall not be subject to any liens against the Property, except for those specified in the Agreement. Buyer shall receive an ALTA-R owner's title insurance policy, if reasonably available. If not, Buyer shall receive a standard coverage owner's policy (e.g. CLTA or ALTA with regional exceptions). Title shall vest as designated in Buyer's escrow instructions. The title company, at Buyer's request, can provide information about availability, desirability, and cost of various title insurance coverages. THE MANNER OF TAKING TITLE MAY HAVE SIGNIFICANT LEGAL AND TAX CONSEQUENCES.

9. CONDITION OF PROPERTY:

A. EXCEPT AS SPECIFIED IN THIS AGREEMENT, Property is sold "AS IS," WITHOUT WARRANTY, in its PRESENT physical condition.

B. (IF CHECKED) SELLER WARRANTS THAT AT THE TIME POSSESSION IS MADE AVAILABLE TO BUYER:

- ☐ **(1)** Roof shall be free of leaks KNOWN to Seller or DISCOVERED during escrow.
- ☐ **(2)** Built-in appliances (including free-standing oven and range, if included in sale), heating, air conditioning, electrical, mechanical, water, sewer, and pool/spa systems, if any, shall be repaired, if KNOWN by Seller to be inoperative or DISCOVERED to be so during escrow. (Well system is not warranted by this paragraph. Well system is covered by paragraphs 4G, 12 and 16.)
- ☐ **(3)** Plumbing systems, shower pans, and shower enclosures shall be free of leaks KNOWN to Seller or DISCOVERED during escrow.
- ☐ **(4)** All fire, safety, and structural defects in chimneys and fireplaces KNOWN to Seller or DISCOVERED during escrow shall be repaired.
- ☐ **(5)** Septic system, if any, shall be repaired, if KNOWN by Seller to be inoperative, or DISCOVERED to be so during escrow.
- ☐ **(6)** All broken or cracked glass, torn existing window and door screens, and multi-pane windows with broken seals, shall be replaced.
- ☐ **(7)** All debris and all personal property not included in the sale shall be removed.
- ☐ **(8)** _____

C. PROPERTY MAINTENANCE: Unless otherwise agreed, Property, including pool, spa, landscaping and grounds, is to be maintained in substantially the same condition as on the date of Acceptance.

D. INSPECTIONS AND DISCLOSURES: Items discovered in Buyer's Inspections which are not covered by paragraph 9B, shall be governed by the procedure in paragraphs 12 and 16. Buyer retains the right to disapprove the condition of the Property based upon items discovered in Buyer's Inspections. Disclosures in the TDS and items discovered in Buyer's Inspections do NOT eliminate Seller's obligations under paragraph 9B, unless specifically agreed in writing. WHETHER OR NOT SELLER WARRANTS ANY ASPECT OF THE PROPERTY, SELLER IS OBLIGATED TO DISCLOSE KNOWN MATERIAL FACTS, AND TO MAKE OTHER DISCLOSURES REQUIRED BY LAW

Buyer and Seller acknowledge receipt of copy of this page, which constitutes Page 2 of _____ Pages.
Buyer's Initials (_____) (_____) Seller's Initials (_____) (_____)

OFFICE USE ONLY
Reviewed by Broker or Designee _____
Date _____

REVISED 4/98

RESIDENTIAL PURCHASE AGREEMENT AND RECEIPT FOR DEPOSIT (RPA-14 PAGE 2 OF 5)

Property Address: _____ **Date:** _____

10. **FIXTURES:** All EXISTING fixtures and fittings that are attached to the Property, or for which special openings have been made, are INCLUDED IN THE PURCHASE PRICE (unless excluded below), and shall be transferred free of liens and "AS IS," unless specifically warranted. Fixtures shall include, but are not limited to, existing electrical, mechanical, lighting, plumbing and heating fixtures, fireplace inserts, solar systems, built-in appliances, window and door screens, awnings, shutters, window coverings, attached floor coverings, television antennas, satellite dishes and related equipment, private integrated telephone systems, air coolers/conditioners, pool/spa equipment, garage door openers/remote controls, attached fireplace equipment, mailbox, in-ground landscaping, including trees/shrubs, and (if owned by Seller) water softeners, water purifiers and security systems/alarms, and _____.
    FIXTURES EXCLUDED: _____.

11. **PERSONAL PROPERTY:** The following items of personal property, free of liens and "AS IS," unless specifically warranted, are INCLUDED IN THE PURCHASE PRICE: _____.

12. **BUYER'S INVESTIGATION OF PROPERTY CONDITION:** Buyer's Acceptance of the condition of the Property is a contingency of this Agreement, as specified in this paragraph and paragraph 16. Buyer shall have the right, at Buyer's expense, to conduct inspections, investigations, tests, surveys, and other studies ("Inspections"), including the right to inspect for lead-based paint and other lead hazards. No Inspections shall be made by any governmental building or zoning inspector, or government employee, without Seller's prior written consent, unless required by Law. Property improvements may not be built according to codes or in compliance with current Law, or have had permits issued. Buyer shall, within the time specified in Paragraph 16A(2), complete these Inspections and notify Seller in writing of any items reasonably disapproved. Seller shall make Property available for all Inspections. Buyer shall: keep Property free and clear of liens; indemnify and hold Seller harmless from all liability, claims, demands, damages and costs; and repair all damages arising from Inspections. Buyer shall carry, or Buyer shall require anyone acting on Buyer's behalf to carry, policies of liability, worker's compensation, and other applicable insurance, defending and protecting Seller from liability for any injuries to persons or property occurring during any work done on the Property at Buyer's direction, prior to Close Of Escrow. Seller is advised that certain protections may be afforded Seller by recording a notice of non-responsibility for work done on the Property at Buyer's direction. At Seller's request, Buyer shall give Seller, at no cost, complete copies of all Inspection reports obtained by Buyer concerning the Property. Seller shall have water, gas, and electricity on for Buyer's Inspections, and through the date possession is made available to Buyer.

13. **FINAL WALK-THROUGH; VERIFICATION OF CONDITION:** Buyer shall have the right to make a final inspection of the Property within 5 (or ☐ _____) Days prior to Close Of Escrow, NOT AS A CONTINGENCY OF THE SALE, but solely to confirm that Repairs have been completed as agreed in writing, and that Seller has complied with Seller's other obligations.

14. **PRORATIONS AND PROPERTY TAXES:** Unless otherwise agreed in writing, real property taxes and assessments, interest, rents, HOA regular, special, and emergency dues and assessments imposed prior to Close of Escrow, premiums on insurance assumed by Buyer, payments on bonds and assessments assumed by Buyer, and payments on Mello-Roos and other Special Assessment District bonds and assessments which are now a lien shall be PAID CURRENT and prorated between Buyer and Seller as of Close Of Escrow. Prorated payments on Mello-Roos and other Special Assessment District bonds and assessments and HOA special assessments that are now a lien but not yet due, shall be assumed by Buyer WITHOUT CREDIT toward the purchase price. Property will be reassessed upon change of ownership. Any supplemental tax bills shall be paid as follows: **(1)** For periods after Close Of Escrow, by Buyer; and, **(2)** For periods prior to Close Of Escrow, by Seller. TAX BILLS ISSUED AFTER CLOSE OF ESCROW SHALL BE HANDLED DIRECTLY BETWEEN BUYER AND SELLER. Exceptions: _____
_____.

15. **SALE OF BUYER'S PROPERTY:**
    A. This Agreement is NOT contingent upon the sale of Buyer's property, unless paragraph 15B is checked.

OR **B.** ☐ (If checked) This Agreement IS CONTINGENT on the Close Of Escrow of Buyer's property, described as (address) _____
_____ ("Buyer's Property"), which is
(if checked) ☐ listed for sale with _____ Company, and/or
(if checked) ☐ in Escrow No. _____ with _____ Escrow Holder, scheduled to
Close Escrow on _____ (date). Buyer shall deliver to Seller, within **5 Days** After Seller's request, a copy of the contract for the sale of Buyer's Property, escrow instructions, and all amendments and modifications thereto. If Buyer's Property does not close escrow by the date specified for Close Of Escrow in this paragraph, then either Seller or Buyer may cancel this Agreement in writing.

After Acceptance:

(1) (Applies UNLESS (2) is checked): Seller SHALL have the right to continue to offer the Property for sale. If Seller accepts another written offer, Seller shall give Buyer written notice to **(i)** remove this contingency in writing, **(ii)** provide written verification of sufficient funds to close escrow on this sale without the sale of Buyer's Property, and **(iii)** comply with the following additional requirement(s) _____

_____.

If Buyer fails to complete those actions within **72 (or ☐ _____) hours** After receipt of such notice, Seller may cancel this Agreement in writing.

OR ☐ **(2) (APPLIES ONLY IF CHECKED:)** Seller SHALL NOT have the right to continue to offer the Property for sale, except for back-up offers.

16. **TIME PERIODS/DISAPPROVAL RIGHTS/REMOVAL OF CONTINGENCIES/CANCELLATION RIGHTS:**

A. **TIME PERIODS:** The following time periods shall apply, unless changed by mutual written agreement:

(1) **SELLER HAS: 5 (or ☐ _____) Days** After Acceptance to, as applicable, order, request or complete, and **2 Days** After receipt (or completion) to provide to Buyer all reports, disclosures, and information for which Seller is responsible under paragraphs 4, 6, 7, and 8.

(2) **BUYER HAS: (a) 10 (or ☐ _____) Days** After Acceptance to complete all inspections, investigations and review of reports and other applicable information for which Buyer is responsible,(including Inspections for lead-based paint and other lead hazards under paragraph 12), with an additional **7 Days** to complete geologic Inspections. WITHIN THIS TIME, Buyer must either disapprove in writing any items, (including, if applicable, the pest control Report under paragraph 4O(1)) which are unacceptable to Buyer, or remove any contingency or disapproval right associated with that item by the active or passive method, as specified below; **(b) 5 (or ☐ _____) Days** After receipt of **(i)** each of the items in paragraph 16A(1); and **(ii)** notice of code and legal violations under paragraph 7D, to either disapprove in writing any items which are unacceptable to Buyer, or to remove any contingency or disapproval right associated with that item, by the active or passive method, as specified below.

(3) **SELLER'S RESPONSE TO BUYER'S DISAPPROVALS:** Seller shall have **5 (or ☐ _____) Days** After receipt of Buyer's written notice of items reasonably disapproved, to respond in writing. If Seller refuses or is unable to make repairs to, or correct, any items reasonably disapproved by Buyer, or if Seller does not respond within the time period specified, Buyer shall have **5 (or ☐ _____) Days** After receipt of Seller's response, or after the expiration of the time for Seller to respond, whichever occurs first, to cancel this Agreement in writing.

B. **ACTIVE OR PASSIVE REMOVAL OF BUYER'S CONTINGENCIES:**

(1) ☐ **ACTIVE METHOD (APPLIES IF CHECKED):** If Buyer does not give Seller written notice of items reasonably disapproved, removal of contingencies or disapproval right, or notice of cancellation within the time periods specified, Seller shall have the right to cancel this Agreement by giving written notice to Buyer.

(2) **PASSIVE METHOD (Applies UNLESS Active Method is checked):** If Buyer does not give Seller written notice of items reasonably disapproved, or of removal of contingencies or disapproval right, or notice of cancellation within the time periods specified, Buyer shall be deemed to have removed and waived any contingency or disapproval right, or the right to cancel, associated with that item.

C. **EFFECT OF CONTINGENCY REMOVAL:** If Buyer removes any contingency or cancellation right by the active or passive method, as applicable, Buyer shall conclusively be deemed to have: **(1)** Completed all Inspections, investigations, and review of reports and other applicable information and disclosures pertaining to that contingency or cancellation right; **(2)** Elected to proceed with the transaction; and, **(3)** Assumed all liability, responsibility, and expense for repairs or corrections pertaining to that contingency or cancellation right, or for inability to obtain financing if the contingency pertains to financing, except for items which Seller has agreed in writing to repair or correct.

Buyer and Seller acknowledge receipt of copy of this page, which constitutes Page 3 of _____ Pages.

Buyer's Initials (_____) (_____)   Seller's Initials (_____) (_____)

REVISED 4/98

OFFICE USE ONLY
Reviewed by Broker
or Designee _____
Date _____

EQUAL HOUSING
OPPORTUNITY

RESIDENTIAL PURCHASE AGREEMENT AND RECEIPT FOR DEPOSIT (RPA-14 PAGE 3 OF 5)

Property Address: _____ Date: _____

D. CANCELLATION OF SALE/ESCROW; RETURN OF DEPOSITS: If Buyer or Seller gives written NOTICE OF CANCELLATION pursuant to rights duly exercised under the terms of this Agreement, Buyer and Seller agree to sign mutual instructions to cancel the sale and escrow and release deposits, less fees and costs, to the party entitled to the funds. Fees and costs may be payable to service providers and vendors for services and products provided during escrow. Release of funds will require mutual, signed release instructions from both Buyer and Seller, judicial decision, or arbitration award. **A party may be subject to a civil penalty of up to $1,000 for refusal to sign such instructions, if no good faith dispute exists as to who is entitled to the deposited funds (Civil Code §1057.3).**

17. **REPAIRS:** Repairs under this Agreement shall be completed prior to Close Of Escrow, unless otherwise agreed in writing. Work to be performed at Seller's expense may be performed by Seller or through others, provided that work complies with applicable laws, including governmental permit, inspection, and approval requirements. Repairs shall be performed in a skillful manner with materials of quality comparable to existing materials. It is understood that exact restoration of appearance or cosmetic items following all Repairs may not be possible.

18. **WITHHOLDING TAXES:** Seller and Buyer agree to execute and deliver any instrument, affidavit, statement, or instruction reasonably necessary to comply with federal (FIRPTA) and California withholding Laws, if required (such as C.A.R. Forms AS-11 and AB-11).

19. **KEYS:** At the time possession is made available to Buyer, Seller shall provide keys and/or means to operate all Property locks, mailboxes, security systems, alarms, and garage door openers. If the Property is a unit in a condominium or subdivision, Buyer may be required to pay a deposit to the HOA to obtain keys to accessible HOA facilities.

20. **LIQUIDATED DAMAGES: If Buyer fails to complete this purchase by reason of any default of Buyer, Seller shall retain, as liquidated damages for breach of contract, the deposit actually paid. However, if the Property is a dwelling with no more than four units, one of which Buyer intends to occupy, then the amount retained shall be no more than 3% of the purchase price. Any excess shall be returned to Buyer. Buyer and Seller shall also sign a separate liquidated damages provision for any increased deposit. (C.A.R. Form RID-11 shall fulfill this requirement.)** Buyer's Initials _____/_____ Seller's Initials _____/_____

21. **DISPUTE RESOLUTION:**
    A. **MEDIATION:** Buyer and Seller agree to mediate any dispute or claim arising between them out of this Agreement, or any resulting transaction, before resorting to arbitration or court action, subject to paragraphs 21C and D below. Mediation fees, if any, shall be divided equally among the parties involved. If any party commences an action based on a dispute or claim to which this paragraph applies, without first attempting to resolve the matter through mediation, then that party shall not be entitled to recover attorney's fees, even if they would otherwise be available to that party in any such action. THIS MEDIATION PROVISION APPLIES WHETHER OR NOT THE ARBITRATION PROVISION IS INITIALED.
    B. **ARBITRATION OF DISPUTES: Buyer and Seller agree that any dispute or claim in Law or equity arising between them out of this Agreement or any resulting transaction, which is not settled through mediation, shall be decided by neutral, binding arbitration, subject to paragraphs 21C and D below. The arbitrator shall be a retired judge or justice, or an attorney with at least 5 years of residential real estate Law experience, unless the parties mutually agree to a different arbitrator, who shall render an award in accordance with substantive California Law. In all other respects, the arbitration shall be conducted in accordance with Part III, Title 9 of the California Code of Civil Procedure. Judgment upon the award of the arbitrator(s) may be entered in any court having jurisdiction. The parties shall have the right to discovery in accordance with Code of Civil Procedure §1283.05.**

    "NOTICE: BY INITIALING IN THE SPACE BELOW YOU ARE AGREEING TO HAVE ANY DISPUTE ARISING OUT OF THE MATTERS INCLUDED IN THE 'ARBITRATION OF DISPUTES' PROVISION DECIDED BY NEUTRAL ARBITRATION AS PROVIDED BY CALIFORNIA LAW AND YOU ARE GIVING UP ANY RIGHTS YOU MIGHT POSSESS TO HAVE THE DISPUTE LITIGATED IN A COURT OR JURY TRIAL. BY INITIALING IN THE SPACE BELOW YOU ARE GIVING UP YOUR JUDICIAL RIGHTS TO DISCOVERY AND APPEAL, UNLESS THOSE RIGHTS ARE SPECIFICALLY INCLUDED IN THE 'ARBITRATION OF DISPUTES' PROVISION. IF YOU REFUSE TO SUBMIT TO ARBITRATION AFTER AGREEING TO THIS PROVISION, YOU MAY BE COMPELLED TO ARBITRATE UNDER THE AUTHORITY OF THE CALIFORNIA CODE OF CIVIL PROCEDURE. YOUR AGREEMENT TO THIS ARBITRATION PROVISION IS VOLUNTARY."

    "WE HAVE READ AND UNDERSTAND THE FOREGOING AND AGREE TO SUBMIT DISPUTES ARISING OUT OF THE MATTERS INCLUDED IN THE 'ARBITRATION OF DISPUTES' PROVISION TO NEUTRAL ARBITRATION." Buyer's Initials _____/_____ Seller's Initials _____/_____

C. **EXCLUSIONS FROM MEDIATION AND ARBITRATION:** The following matters are excluded from Mediation and Arbitration: **(a)** A judicial or non-judicial foreclosure or other action or proceeding to enforce a deed of trust, mortgage, or installment land sale contract as defined in Civil Code §2985; **(b)** An unlawful detainer action; **(c)** The filing or enforcement of a mechanic's lien; **(d)** Any matter which is within the jurisdiction of a probate, small claims, or bankruptcy court; and **(e)** An action for bodily injury or wrongful death, or for latent or patent defects to which Code of Civil Procedure §337.1 or §337.15 applies. The filing of a court action to enable the recording of a notice of pending action, for order of attachment, receivership, injunction, or other provisional remedies, shall not constitute a violation of the mediation and arbitration provisions.

D. **BROKERS:** Buyer and Seller agree to mediate and arbitrate disputes or claims involving either or both Brokers, provided either or both Brokers shall have agreed to such mediation or arbitration, prior to or within a reasonable time after the dispute or claim is presented to Brokers. Any election by either or both Brokers to participate in mediation or arbitration shall not result in Brokers being deemed parties to the Agreement.

22. **DEFINITIONS:** As used in this Agreement:

A. **"Acceptance"** means the time the offer or final counter offer is accepted in writing by the other party, in accordance with this Agreement or the terms of the final counter offer.

B. **"Agreement"** means the terms and conditions of this Residential Purchase Agreement and any counter offer.

C. **"Days"** means calendar days, unless otherwise required by Law.

D. **"Days After . ."** means the specified number of calendar days after the occurrence of the event specified, not counting the calendar date on which the specified event occurs.

E. **"Close Of Escrow"** means the date the grant deed, or other evidence of transfer of title, is recorded.

F. **"Law"** means any law, code, statute, ordinance, regulation, or rule, which is adopted by a controlling city, county, state or federal legislative or judicial body or agency.

G. **"Repairs"** means any repairs, alterations, replacements, or modifications, (including pest control work) of the Property.

H. **"Pest Control Certification"** means a written statement made by a registered structural pest control company that on the date of inspection or re-inspection, the Property is "free" or is "now free" of "evidence of active infestation in the visible and accessible areas".

I. **Section 1** means infestation or infection which is evident. **Section 2** means present conditions likely to lead to infestation or infection.

J. **Singular and Plural** terms each include the other, when appropriate.

K. **C.A.R. Form** means the specific form referenced, or another comparable form agreed to by the parties.

23. **MULTIPLE LISTING SERVICE ("MLS"):** Brokers are authorized to report the terms of this transaction to any MLS, to be published and disseminated to persons and entities authorized to use the information, on terms approved by the MLS.

Buyer and Seller acknowledge receipt of copy of this page, which constitutes Page 4 of _____ Pages.

Buyer's Initials (_____) (_____)   Seller's Initials (_____) (_____)

REVISED 4/98

OFFICE USE ONLY
Reviewed by Broker
or Designee _____
Date _____

EQUAL HOUSING
OPPORTUNITY

RESIDENTIAL PURCHASE AGREEMENT AND RECEIPT FOR DEPOSIT (RPA-14 PAGE 4 OF 5)

Property Address: _____ **Date:** _____

24. **EQUAL HOUSING OPPORTUNITY:** The Property is sold in compliance with federal, state, and local anti-discrimination Laws.

25. **ATTORNEY'S FEES:** In any action, proceeding, or arbitration between Buyer and Seller arising out of this Agreement, the prevailing Buyer or Seller shall be entitled to reasonable attorney's fees and costs from the non-prevailing Buyer or Seller, except as provided in paragraph 21A.

26. **SELECTION OF SERVICE PROVIDERS:** If Brokers give Buyer or Seller referrals to persons, vendors, or service or product providers ("Providers"), Brokers do not guarantee the performance of any of those Providers. Buyer and Seller may select ANY Providers of their own choosing.

27. **TIME OF ESSENCE; ENTIRE CONTRACT; CHANGES:** Time is of the essence. All understandings between the parties are incorporated in this Agreement. Its terms are intended by the parties as a final, complete, and exclusive expression of their agreement with respect to its subject matter, and may not be contradicted by evidence of any prior agreement or contemporaneous oral agreement. **This Agreement may not be extended, amended, modified, altered, or changed, except in writing signed by Buyer and Seller.**

28. **OTHER TERMS AND CONDITIONS,** including ATTACHED SUPPLEMENTS:
    - ☑ Buyer Inspection Advisory (C.A.R. Form BIA-14)
    - ☐ Purchase Agreement Addendum (C.A.R. Form PAA-14 paragraph numbers: _____)
    - _____
    - _____
    - _____

29. **AGENCY CONFIRMATION:** The following agency relationships are hereby confirmed for this transaction:
    Listing Agent: _____ (Print Firm Name) is the agent of (check one):
    - ☐ the Seller exclusively; or ☐ both the Buyer and Seller.
    Selling Agent: _____ (Print Firm Name) (if not same as Listing Agent) is the agent of (check one):
    - ☐ the Buyer exclusively; or ☐ the Seller exclusively; or ☐ both the Buyer and Seller.
    Real Estate Brokers are not parties to the Agreement between Buyer and Seller.

30. **OFFER:** This is an offer to purchase the Property on the above terms and conditions. All paragraphs with spaces for initials by Buyer and Seller are incorporated in this Agreement only if initialed by all parties. If at least one but not all parties initial, a counter offer is required until agreement is reached. Unless Acceptance of Offer is signed by Seller, and a signed copy delivered in person, by mail, or facsimile, and personally received by Buyer, or by _____, who is authorized to receive it, by (date) _____, at _____ AM/PM, the offer shall be deemed revoked and the deposit shall be returned. Buyer has read and acknowledges receipt of a copy of the offer and agrees to the above confirmation of agency relationships. If this offer is accepted and Buyer subsequently defaults, Buyer may be responsible for payment of Brokers' compensation. This Agreement and any supplement, addendum, or modification, including any photocopy or facsimile, may be signed in two or more counterparts, all of which shall constitute one and the same writing.

Buyer and Seller acknowledge and agree that Brokers: (a) Do not decide what price Buyer should pay or Seller should accept; (b) Do not guarantee the condition of the Property; (c) Shall not be responsible for defects that are not known to Broker(s) and are not visually observable in reasonably accessible areas of the Property; (d) Do not guarantee the performance or Repairs of others who have provided services or products to Buyer or Seller; (e) Cannot identify Property boundary lines; (f) Cannot verify inspection reports, square footage or representations of others; (g) Cannot provide legal or tax advice; (h) Will not provide other advice or information that exceeds the knowledge, education and experience required to obtain a real estate license. Buyer and Seller agree that they will seek legal, tax, insurance, and other desired assistance from appropriate professionals.

BUYER _____   BUYER _____

31. **BROKER COMPENSATION:** Seller agrees to pay compensation for services as follows:

_____, to _____, Broker, and
_____, to _____, Broker,

payable: **(a)** On recordation of the deed or other evidence of title; or **(b)** If completion of sale is prevented by default of Seller, upon Seller's default; or, **(c)** If completion of sale is prevented by default of Buyer, only if and when Seller collects damages from Buyer, by suit or otherwise, and then in an amount equal to one-half of the damages recovered, but not to exceed the above compensation, after first deducting title and escrow expenses and the expenses of collection, if any. Seller hereby irrevocably assigns to Brokers such compensation from Seller's proceeds, and irrevocably instructs Escrow Holder to disburse those funds to Brokers at close of escrow. Commission instructions can be amended or revoked only with the written consent of Brokers. In any action, proceeding or arbitration relating to the payment of such compensation, the prevailing party shall be entitled to reasonable attorney's fees and costs, except as provided in paragraph 21A.

32. **ACCEPTANCE OF OFFER:** Seller warrants that Seller is the owner of this Property, or has the authority to execute this Agreement. Seller accepts the above offer, agrees to sell the Property on the above terms and conditions, and agrees to the above confirmation of agency relationships. Seller has read and acknowledges receipt of a copy of this Agreement, and authorizes Broker to deliver a signed copy to Buyer.

If checked: ☐ **SUBJECT TO ATTACHED COUNTER OFFER, DATED** _____

SELLER_____   Date _____

SELLER_____   Date _____

(___/___) **ACKNOWLEDGMENT OF RECEIPT:** Buyer or authorized agent acknowledges receipt of signed Acceptance on (date) _____,
(Initials)   at _____ AM/PM.

Agency relationships are confirmed as above. Real Estate Brokers are not parties to the Agreement between Buyer and Seller.
Receipt for deposit is acknowledged:

Real Estate Broker (Selling Firm Name) _____ By _____ Date _____
Address _____ Telephone _____ Fax _____
Real Estate Broker (Listing Firm Name) _____ By _____ Date _____
Address _____ Telephone _____ Fax _____

This form is available for use by the entire real estate industry. It is not intended to identify the user as a REALTOR®. REALTOR® is a registered collective membership mark which may be used only by members of the NATIONAL ASSOCIATION OF REALTORS® who subscribe to its Code of Ethics.

REVISED 4/98

Page 5 of _____ Pages.

┌─ OFFICE USE ONLY ─┐
Reviewed by Broker
or Designee _____
Date _____

EQUAL HOUSING OPPORTUNITY

RESIDENTIAL PURCHASE AGREEMENT AND RECEIPT FOR DEPOSIT (RPA-14 PAGE 5 OF 5)

Reprinted with permission, California Association of REALTORS®. Endorsement not implied.

INSPECTION RIDER

Address: _____

This Rider is a supplement to and part of the Agreement for Sale of Residential
Real Estate dated _____, between the Seller _____
And the Purchaser _____, to which it is attached.

Prior to closing of this transaction the parties agree that the following listed inspection(s)
shall be made on the property and paid for by the indicated party:

Type of Inspection: _____ paid for by _____
                       _____ paid for by _____
                       _____ paid for by _____
                       _____ paid for by _____
                       _____ paid for by _____
All inspections to be completed on or before: _____

1. If such inspection(s) indicate approval of the condition of the item or items to be
   inspected, this agreement shall remain in full force and effect.

2. If such inspection(s) state disapproval of any item or items to be inspected and notice of
   such disapproval is served on the Seller within 24 hours after completed inspection(s),
   then this agreement shall be terminated and the downpayment shall be returned to the
   Purchaser.

3. Notwithstanding the above, the parties may agree, by amendment and modification to
   this agreement, on the terms necessary to remedy any problem related by inspection,
   and being the cause of disapproval, and to proceed thereunder with performance of this
   agreement.

_____   _____
Purchaser   Seller

_____   _____
Purchaser   Seller

_____   _____
Date   Date

APPENDIX
B

Lead-Based Paint
and
Lead-Based Paint
Hazards Disclosure

CALIFORNIA
ASSOCIATION
OF REALTORS®

LEAD-BASED PAINT AND LEAD-BASED PAINT HAZARDS
DISCLOSURE, ACKNOWLEDGMENT AND ADDENDUM FOR
Pre-1978 Housing Sales, Leases, or Rentals

The following terms and conditions are hereby incorporated in and made a part of the: ☐ Residential Purchase Agreement, ☐ Residential Lease or Month-to-Month Rental Agreement, or ☐ other: _____,
dated _____, on property known as: _____ ("Property")
in which _____ is referred to as Buyer or Tenant
and _____ is referred to as Seller or Landlord.

LEAD WARNING STATEMENT Every purchaser or tenant of any interest in residential real property on which a residential dwelling was built prior to 1978 is notified that such property may present exposure to lead from lead-based paint, paint chips and dust that may place young children at risk of developing lead poisoning. Lead can pose health hazards if not taken care of properly. Lead poisoning in young children may produce permanent neurological damage, including learning disabilities, reduced intelligence quotient, behavioral problems, and impaired memory. Lead poisoning also poses a particular risk to pregnant women. The seller or landlord of any interest in pre-1978 residential real property, prior to the sale or rental, is required to: **(a)** Provide the buyer or tenant with any information on lead-based paint hazards from risk assessments or inspections in the seller or landlord's possession; **(b)** Notify the buyer or tenant of any known lead-based paint hazards; and **(c)** Give the buyer or tenant a Federally approved pamphlet on lead poisoning prevention. A risk assessment or inspection for possible lead-based paint hazards is recommended prior to purchase.

1. SELLER'S OR LANDLORD'S DISCLOSURE

I (we) have no knowledge of lead-based paint and/or lead-based paint hazards in the housing other than the following: _____
_____
_____

I (we) have no reports or records pertaining to lead-based paint and/or lead-based paint hazards in the housing other than the following, which, previously or as an attachment to this addendum have been provided to Buyer or Tenant: _____
_____
_____

I (we), previously or as an attachment to this addendum, have provided Buyer or Tenant with the pamphlet *"Protect Your Family From Lead In Your Home"* or an equivalent pamphlet approved for use in the State such as *"The Homeowner's Guide to Environmental Hazards and Earthquake Safety."*

For Sales Transactions Only: Buyer has 10 days, unless otherwise agreed in the real estate purchase contract, to conduct a risk assessment or inspection for the presence of lead-based paint and/or lead-based paint hazards;

I (we) have reviewed the information above and certify, to the best of my (our) knowledge, that the information provided is true and correct.

_____   _____   _____   _____
Seller or Landlord   Date   Seller or Landlord   Date

2. LISTING AGENT'S ACKNOWLEDGMENT

Agent has informed Seller or Landlord of Seller's or Landlord's obligations under §42 U.S.C. 4852d and is aware of Agent's responsibility to ensure compliance.

I have reviewed the information above and certify, to the best of my knowledge, that the information provided is true and correct.

_____ By _____

Agent (Broker representing Seller) Please Print   Associate Licensee or Broker-Signature   Date

3. BUYER'S OR TENANT'S ACKNOWLEDGMENT

I (we) have received copies of all information listed, if any, in 1 above and the pamphlet "*Protect Your Family From Lead In Your Home*" or an equivalent pamphlet approved for use in the State such as "*The Homeowner's Guide to Environmental Hazards and Earthquake Safety.*"

For Sales Transactions Only: Buyer acknowledges the right for 10 days, unless otherwise agreed in the real estate purchase contract, to conduct a risk assessment or inspection for the presence of lead-based paint and/or lead-based paint hazards; OR, (if checked) ☐ Buyer waives the right to conduct a risk assessment or inspection for the presence of lead-based paint and/or lead-based paint hazards.

I (we) have reviewed the information above and certify, to the best of my (our) knowledge, that the information provided is true and correct.

_____   _____

Buyer or Tenant   Date   Buyer or Tenant   Date

4. COOPERATING AGENT'S ACKNOWLEDGMENT

Agent has informed Seller or Landlord, through the Listing Agent if the property is listed, of Seller's or Landlord's obligations under §42 USC 4852d and is aware of Agent's responsibility to ensure compliance.

I have reviewed the information above and certify, to the best of my knowledge, that the information provided is true and correct.

_____ By _____

Agent (Broker obtaining the Offer)   Associate Licensee or Broker-Signature   Date

REBS   Published and Distributed by:
REAL ESTATE BUSINESS SERVICES, INC.
a subsidiary of the CALIFORNIA ASSOCIATION OF REALTORS®
525 South Virgil Avenue, Los Angeles, California 90020

PRINT DATE

OFFICE USE ONLY
Reviewed by Broker
or Designee _____
Date _____

EQUAL HOUSING OPPORTUNITY

FORM FLD-14 REVISED 10/97

UNITED STATES CODE TITLE 42 SECTION 4852d
reads in part . . .

§4852d. Disclosure of information concerning lead upon transfer of residential property.

(a) **Lead disclosure in purchase and sale or lease of target housing.** (1) Lead-based paint hazards. Not later than 2 years after the date of enactment of this Act [enacted Oct. 28, 1992], the Secretary and the Administrator of the Environmental Protection Agency shall promulgate regulations under this section for the disclosure of lead-based paint hazards in target housing which is offered for sale or lease. The regulations shall require that, before the purchaser or lessee is obligated under any contract to purchase or lease the housing, the seller or lessor shall

    (A)   provide the purchaser or lessee with a lead hazard information pamphlet, . . .;

    (B)   disclose to the purchaser or lessee the presence of any known lead-based paint, or any known lead-based paint hazards, in such housing and provide to the purchaser or lessee any lead hazard evaluation report available to the seller or lessor; and

    (C)   permit the purchaser a 10-day period (unless the parties mutually agree upon a different period of time) to conduct a risk assessment or inspection for the presence of lead-based paint hazards.

(2) Contract for purchase and sale. Regulations promulgated under this section shall provide that every contract or the purchase and sale of any interest in target housing shall contain a Lead Warning Statement and a statement signed by the purchaser that the purchaser has

    (A)   read the Lead Warning Statement and understands its contents;

    (B)   received a lead hazard information pamphlet; and

    (C)   had a 10-day opportunity (unless the parties mutually agreed upon a different period of time) before becoming obligated under the contract to purchase the housing to conduct a risk assessment or inspection for the presence of lead-based paint hazards.

(3) Contents of Lead Warning Statement. The Lead Warning Statement shall contain the following text printed in large type on a separate sheet of paper attached to the contract: 'Every purchaser of any interest in residential real property on which a residential dwelling was built prior to 1978 is notified that such property may present exposure to lead from lead-based paint that may place young children at risk of developing lead poisoning. Lead poisoning in young children may produce permanent neurological damage, including learning disabilities, reduced intelligence quotient, behavioral problems, and impaired memory. Lead poisoning also poses a particular risk to pregnant women. The seller of any interest in residential real property is required to provide the buyer with any information on lead-based paint hazards from risk assessments or inspections in the seller's possession and notify the buyer of any known lead-based paint hazards. A risk assessment or inspection for possible lead-based paint hazards is recommended prior to purchase.'

(4) Compliance assurance. Whenever a seller or lessor has entered into a contract with an agent for the purpose of selling or leasing a unit of target housing, the regulations promulgated under this section shall require the agent, on behalf of the seller or lessor, to ensure compliance with the requirements of this section.

(Oct. 28, 1992, P.L. 102-550, Title X, Subtitle A, § 1018, 106 Stat. 3910.)

APPENDIX

C

Disclosure Regarding Real Estate Agency Relationships

CALIFORNIA
ASSOCIATION
OF REALTORS®

DISCLOSURE REGARDING
REAL ESTATE AGENCY RELATIONSHIPS
(As required by the Civil Code)

When you enter into a discussion with a real estate agent regarding a real estate transaction, you should from the outset understand what type of agency relationship or representation you wish to have with the agent in the transaction.

SELLER'S AGENT

A Seller's agent under a listing agreement with the Seller acts as the agent for the Seller only. A Seller's agent or a subagent of that agent has the following affirmative obligations:
To the Seller:
   A Fiduciary duty of utmost care, integrity, honesty, and loyalty in dealings with the Seller.
To the Buyer and the Seller:
   (a) Diligent exercise of reasonable skill and care in performance of the agent's duties.
   (b) A duty of honest and fair dealing and good faith.
   (c) A duty to disclose all facts known to the agent materially affecting the value or desirability of the property that are not known to, or within the diligent attention and observation of, the parties.

An agent is not obligated to reveal to either party any confidential information obtained from the other party that does not involve the affirmative duties set forth above.

BUYER'S AGENT

A selling agent can, with a Buyer's consent, agree to act as agent for the Buyer only. In these situations, the agent is not the Seller's agent, even if by agreement the agent may receive compensation for services rendered, either in full or in part from the Seller. An agent acting only for a Buyer has the following affirmative obligations:
To the Buyer:
   A fiduciary duty of utmost care, integrity, honesty, and loyalty in dealings with the Buyer.
To the Buyer and the Seller:
   (a) Diligent exercise of reasonable skill and care in performance of the agent's duties.
   (b) A duty of honest and fair dealing and good faith.
   (c) A duty to disclose all facts known to the agent materially affecting the value or desirability of the property that are not known to, or within the diligent attention and observation of, the parties.

An agent is not obligated to reveal to either party any confidential information obtained from the other party that does not involve the affirmative duties set forth above.

AGENT REPRESENTING BOTH SELLER & BUYER

A real estate agent, either acting directly or through one or more associate licensees can legally be the agent of both the Seller and the Buyer in a transaction, but only with the knowledge and consent of both the Seller and the Buyer.

In a dual agency situation, the agent has the following affirmative obligations to both the Seller and the Buyer:
   (a) A fiduciary duty of utmost care, integrity, honest and loyalty in the dealings with either Seller or the Buyer.
   (b) Other duties to the Seller and the Buyer as stated above in their respective sections.

In representing both Seller and Buyer, the agent may not, without the express permission of the respective party, disclose to the other party that the Seller will accept a price less than the listing price or that the Buyer will pay a price greater than the price offered.

The above duties of the agent in a real estate transaction do not relieve a Seller or Buyer from the responsibility to protect his or her own interests. You should carefully read all agreements to assure that they adequately express your understanding of the transaction. A real estate agent is a person qualified to advise about real estate. If legal or tax advice is desired, consult a competent professional.

Throughout your real property transaction you may receive more than one disclosure form, depending upon the number of agents assisting in the transaction. The law requires each agent with whom you have more than a casual relationship to present you with this disclosure form. You should read its contents each time it is presented to you, considering the relationship between you and the real estate agent in your specific transaction.

This disclosure form includes the provisions of Sections 2079.13 to 2079.24, inclusive, of the Civil Code set forth on the reverse hereof. Read it carefully.

I/WE ACKNOWLEDGE RECEIPT OF A COPY OF THIS DISCLOSURE.

BUYER/SELLER _____ Date _____ Time _____ AM/PM

BUYER/SELLER _____ Date _____ Time _____ AM/PM

AGENT _____ By _____ Date _____
(Please Print)   (Associate Licensee or Broker-Signature)

This Disclosure form must be provided in a listing, sale, exchange, installment land contract, or lease over one year, if the transaction involves one-to-four dwelling residential property, including a mobile home, as follows:
(a) From a Listing Agent to a Seller: Prior to entering into the listing.
(b) From an Agent selling a property he/she has listed to a Buyer: Prior to the Buyer's execution of the offer.
(c) From a Selling Agent to a Buyer: Prior to the Buyer's execution of the offer.
(d) From a Selling Agent (in a cooperating real estate firm) to a Seller: Prior to presentation of the offer to the Seller.

It is not necessary or required to confirm an agency relationship using a separate Confirmation form if the agency confirmation portion of the Real Estate Purchase Contract is properly completed in full. However, it is still necessary to use this Disclosure form.

THIS FORM HAS BEEN APPROVED BY THE CALIFORNIA ASSOCIATION OF REALTORS® (C.A.R.). NO REPRESENTATION IS MADE AS TO THE LEGAL VALIDITY OR ADEQUACY OF ANY PROVISION IN ANY SPECIFIC TRANSACTION. A REAL ESTATE BROKER IS THE PERSON QUALIFIED TO ADVISE ON REAL ESTATE TRANSACTIONS. IF YOU DESIRE LEGAL OR TAX ADVICE, CONSULT AN APPROPRIATE PROFESSIONAL.

This form is available for use by the entire real estate industry. It is not intended to identify the user as a REALTOR®. REALTOR® is a registered collective membership mark which may be used only by members of the NATIONAL ASSOCIATION OF REALTORS® who subscribe to its Code of Ethics.

The copyright laws of the United States (17 U.S. Code) forbid the unauthorized reproduction of this form by any means, including facsimile or computerized formats. Copyright © 1987-1997, CALIFORNIA ASSOCIATION OF REALTORS®

| R E B S | Published and Distributed by: REAL ESTATE BUSINESS SERVICES, INC. a subsidiary of the CALIFORNIA ASSOCIATION OF REALTORS® 525 South Virgil Avenue, Los Angeles, California 90020 | OFFICE USE ONLY Reviewed by Broker or Designee _____ Date _____ | EQUAL HOUSING OPPORTUNITY |

FORM AD-14 REVISED 10/95

CHAPTER 2 OF TITLE 9 OF PART 4 OF DIVISION 3 OF THE CIVIL CODE

2079.13   As used in Sections 2079.14 to 2079.24, inclusive, the following terms have the following meanings:

(a) "Agent" means a person acting under provisions of title 9 (commencing with Section 2295) in a real property transaction, and includes a person who is licensed as a real estate broker under Chapter 3 (commencing with Section 10130) of Part 1 of Division 4 of the Business and Professions Code, and under whose license a listing is executed or an offer to purchase is obtained.

(b) "Associate licensee" means a person who is licensed as a real broker or salesperson under Chapter 3 (commencing with Section 10130) of Part 1 of Division 4 of the Business and Professions Code and who is either licensed under a broker or has entered into a written contract with a broker to act as the broker's agent in connection with acts requiring a real estate license and to function under the broker's supervision in the capacity of an associate licensee.

The agent in the real property transaction bears responsibility for his or her associate licensees who perform as agents of the agent. When an associate licensee owes a duty to any principal, or to any buyer or seller who is not a principal, in a real property transaction, that duty is equivalent to the duty owed to that party by the broker for whom the associate licensee functions.

(c) "Buyer" means a transferee in a real property transaction, and includes a person who executes an offer to purchase real property from a seller through an agent, or who seeks the services of an agent in more than a casual, transitory, or preliminary manner, with the object of entering into a real property transaction. "Buyer" includes vendee or lessee.

(d) "Dual agent" means an agent acting, either directly or through an associate licensee, as agent for both the seller and the buyer in a real property transaction.

(e) "Listing agreement" means a contract between an owner of real property and an agent, by which the agent has been authorized to sell the real property or to find or obtain a buyer.

(f) "Listing agent" means a person who has obtained a listing of real property to act as an agent for compensation.

(g) "Listing price" is the amount expressed in dollars specified in the listing for which the seller is willing to sell the real property through the listing agent.

(h) "Offering price" is the amount expressed in dollars specified in an offer to purchase for which the buyer is willing to buy the real property.

(i) "Offer to purchase" means a written contract executed by a buyer acting through a selling agent which becomes the contract for the sale of the real property upon acceptance by the seller.

(j) "Real property" means any estate specified by subdivision (1) or (2) of Section 761 in property which constitutes or is improved with one to four dwelling units, any leasehold in this type of property exceeding one year's duration, and mobilehomes, when offered for sale or sold through an agent pursuant to the authority contained in Section 10131.6 of the Business and Professions Code.

(k) "Real property transaction" means a transaction for the sale of real property in which an agent is employed by one or more of the principals to act in that transaction, and includes a listing or an offer to purchase.

(l) "Sell," "sale," or "sold" refers to a transaction for the transfer of real property from the seller to the buyer, and includes exchanges of real property between the seller and buyer, transactions for the creation of a real property sales contract within the meaning of Section 2985, and transactions for the creation of a leasehold exceeding one year's duration.

(m) "Seller" means the transferor in a real property transaction, and includes an owner who lists real property with an agent, whether or not a transfer results, or who receives an offer to purchase real property of which he or she is the owner from an agent on behalf of another. "Seller" includes both a vendor and a lessor.

(n) "Selling agent" means a listing agent who acts alone, or an agent who acts in cooperation with a listing agent, and who sells or finds and obtains a buyer for the real property, or an agent who locates property for a buyer or who finds a buyer for a property for which no listing exists and presents an offer to purchase to the seller.

(o) "Subagent" means a person to whom an agent delegates agency powers as provided in Article 5 (commencing with Section 2349) of Chapter 1 of Title 9. However, "subagent" does not include an associate licensee who is acting under the supervision of an agent in a real property transaction.

2079.14 Listing agents and selling agents shall provide the seller and buyer in a real property transaction with a copy of the disclosure form specified in Section 2079.16, and, except as provided in subdivision (c), shall obtain a signed acknowledgement of receipt from that seller or buyer, except as provided in this section or Section 2079.15, as follows:

(a) The listing agent, if any, shall provide the disclosure form to the seller prior to entering into the listing agreement.

(b) The selling agent shall provide the disclosure form to the seller as soon as practicable prior to presenting the seller with an offer to purchase, unless the selling agent previously provided the seller with a copy of the disclosure form pursuant to subdivision (a).

(c) Where the selling agent does not deal on a face-to-face basis with the seller, the disclosure form prepared by the selling agent may be furnished to the seller (and acknowledgement of receipt obtained for the selling agent from the seller) by the listing agent, or the selling agent may deliver the disclosure form by certified mail addressed to the seller at his or her last known address, in which case no signed acknowledgement of receipt is required.

(d) The selling agent shall provide the disclosure form to the buyer as soon as practicable prior to execution of the buyer's offer to purchase, except that if the offer to purchase is not prepared by the selling agent, the selling agent shall present the disclosure form to the buyer not later than the next business day after the selling agent receives the offer to purchase from the buyer.

2079.15 In any circumstance in which the seller or buyer refuses to sign an acknowledgement of receipt pursuant to Section 2079.14, the agent, or an associate licensee acting for an agent, shall set forth, sign, and date a written declaration of the facts of the refusal.

2079.17 (a) As soon as practicable, the selling agent shall disclose to the buyer and seller whether the selling agent is acting in the real property transaction exclusively as the buyer's agent, exclusively as the seller's agent, or as a dual agent representing both the buyer and the seller. This relationship shall be confirmed in the contract to purchase and sell real property or in a separate writing executed or acknowledged by the seller, the buyer, and the selling agent prior to or coincident with execution of that contract by the buyer and the seller, respectively.

(b) As soon as practicable, the listing agent shall disclose to the seller whether the listing agent is acting in the real property transaction exclusively as the seller's agent, or as a dual agent representing both the buyer and seller. This relationship shall be confirmed in the contract to purchase and sell real property or in a separate writing executed or acknowledged by the seller and the listing agent prior to or coincident with the execution of that contract by the seller.

(c) The confirmation required by subdivisions (a) and (b) shall be in the following form.

_____ is the agent of (check one):   _____ is the agent of (check one):
(Name of Listing Agent)   (Name of Selling Agent if not the same as the Listing Agent)

☐ the seller exclusively; or   ☐ the buyer exclusively; or

☐ both the buyer and seller.   ☐ the seller exclusively; or

                                      ☐ both the buyer and seller.

(d) The disclosures and confirmation required by this section shall be in addition to the disclosure required by Section 2079. 14.

2079.18 No selling agent in a real property transaction may act as an agent for the buyer only, when the selling agent is also acting as the listing agent in the transaction.

2079.19 The payment of compensation or the obligation to pay compensation to an agent by the seller or buyer is not necessarily determinative of a particular agency relationship between an agent and the seller or buyer. A listing agent and a selling agent may agree to share any compensation or commission paid, or any right to any compensation or commission for which an obligation arises as the result of a real estate transaction, and the terms of any such agreement shall not necessarily be determinative of a particular relationship.

2079.20 Nothing in this article prevents an agent from selecting, as a condition of the agent's employment, a specific form of agency relationship not specifically prohibited by this article if the requirements of Section 2079.14 and Section 2079.17 are complied with.

2079.21 A dual agent shall not disclose to the buyer that the seller is willing to sell the property at a price less than the listing price, without the express written consent of the seller. A dual agent shall not disclose to the seller that the buyer is willing to pay a price greater than the offering price, without the express written consent of the buyer.

This section does not alter in any way the duty or responsibility of a dual agent to any principal with respect to confidential information other than price.

2079.22 Nothing in this article precludes a listing agent from also being a selling agent, and the combination of these functions in one agent does not, of itself, make that agent a dual agent.

2079.23 A contract between the principal and agent may be modified or altered to change the agency relationship at any time before the performance of the act which is the object of the agency with the written consent of the parties to the agency relationship.

2079.24 Nothing in this article shall be construed to either diminish the duty of disclosure owed buyers and sellers by agents and their associate licensees, subagents, and employees or to relieve agents and their associate licensees, subagents, and employees from liability for their conduct in connection with acts governed by this article or for any breach of a fiduciary duty or a duty of disclosure.

APPENDIX D

Residential Property Seller Disclosure Statement

RESIDENTIAL PROPERTY SELLER DISCLOSURE STATEMENT

This form approved by the Iowa City Area Association of REALTORS

Property Address:_____

PURPOSE: Use this statement to disclose information as required by Iowa Code chapter 558A. This law requires certain sellers of residential property that includes at least one and no more than four dwelling units to disclose information about the property to be sold. The following disclosures are made by the seller(s) and not by any agent acting on behalf of the seller(s).

INSTRUCTIONS TO SELLER(S): 1) Seller(s) must complete this statement. Complete all questions, or attach reports allowed by Iowa Code section 558A.4(2). 2) Disclose all known conditions materially affecting this property. 3) If an item does not apply to this property, write (NA) not applicable. 4) You must provide information in good faith and make a reasonable effort to ascertain the required information. If the required information is unknown or is unavailable following a reasonable effort, use an approximation of the information and indicate by using (AP), or if the information is unknown, indicate using (UNK). 5) Additional pages may be attached to this form as needed. 6) Keep a copy of this statement with your other important papers.

1. **BASEMENT/FOUNDATION:** Any known past or present water or other problems? ❑ Yes ❑ No If yes, explain _____
   _____Date of repairs _____.

2. **ROOF:** Any known present problems? ❑ Yes ❑ No. If yes, explain _____
   _____Date of repairs/replacement _____.

3. **WELL AND PUMP:** Any known present problems? ❑ Yes ❑ No. If yes, explain _____
   _____Date of repairs/replacement _____.
   Any known water tests? ❑ Yes ❑ No. If yes, date of last report and results_____.

4. **SEPTIC TANKS/DRAIN FIELDS:** Any known present problems? ❑ Yes ❑ No. If yes, explain _____
   _____.
   Location of tank _____Date last cleaned _____.

5. **SEWER SYSTEM:** Any known present problems? ❑ Yes ❑ No. If yes, explain_____
   _____Date of repairs/replacement _____.

6. **HEATING SYSTEMS(S):** Any known present problems? ❑ Yes ❑ No. If yes, explain _____
   _____Date of repairs/replacement _____.

7. **CENTRAL COOLING SYSTEM(S):** Any known present problems? ❑ Yes ❑ No. If yes, explain _____
   _____Date of repairs/replacement _____.

8. **PLUMBING SYSTEM(S):** Any known present problems? ❑ Yes ❑ No. If yes, explain_____
   _____Date of repairs/replacement _____.

9. **ELECTRICAL SYSTEM(S):** Any known present problems? ❑ Yes ❑ No. If yes, explain _____
   _____Date of repairs/replacement _____.

10. **PEST INFESTATION (e.g., termites, carpenter ants):** Any known past or present problems? ❑ Yes ❑ No. If yes, dates of treatment: _____
    Any known structural damage? ❑ Yes ❑ No If yes, date of repairs/replacement _____.

11. **ASBESTOS:** Any known to be present in the structure? ❑ Yes ❑ No. If yes, explain _____
    _____.

11. **ASBESTOS:** Any known to be present in the structure? ❑ Yes ❑ No. If yes, explain _____
_____.

12. **RADON:** Any known tests for the presence of radon gas? ❑ Yes ❑ No. If yes, date of last report_____
Results of last report_____.

13. **LEAD-BASED PAINT:** Was this dwelling constructed prior to January 1, 1978? ❑ Yes ❑ No If yes, complete "Disclosure of Information and Acknowledgement re: Lead-Based Paint and/or Lead-Based Paint Hazards" on the reverse side of this form.

14. **FLOOD PLAIN:** Is the property located in a flood plain? ❑ Yes ❑ No. If yes, what is the flood plain designation? _____
_____.

15. **ZONING:** Do you know the zoning classification of the property? ❑ Yes ❑ No. If yes, what is the zoning classification? _____.

16. **SHARED OR CO-OWNED FEATURES:** Any features of the property known to be shared in common with adjoining landowners, such as walls, fences, roads, and driveways whose use or maintenance responsibility may have an effect on the property? ❑ Yes ❑ No. If yes, explain_____

Any known "common areas" such as pools, tennis courts, walkways, or other areas co-owned with others, or a Homeowner's Association which has authority over the property? ❑ Yes ❑ No. If yes, explain _____.

17. **FLOODING, DRAINING, GRADING:** Any known settling, flooding, drainage or grading problems? ❑ Yes ❑ No. If yes, explain_____
_____.

18. **STRUCTURAL DEFECT:** Any known significant defects in the structural integrity of the structure? ❑ Yes ❑ No. If yes, explain_____
_____.

19. **REAL ESTATE IMPROVEMENT DISTRICT:** Is the property located in a Real Estate Improvement District (REID)? ❑ Yes ❑ No. If yes, what is the amount (if any) of any special assessment against this property? $_____.

YOU MUST EXPLAIN ANY "YES" RESPONSE(S) ABOVE. USE THE BACK OF THIS STATEMENT OR ADDITIONAL SHEETS AS NECESSARY.

SELLER(S) DISCLOSURE STATEMENT IS NOT REQUIRED IN THE FOLLOWING INSTANCES: 1) The property contains no dwelling units or more than 4 dwelling units. 2) The transfer is made pursuant to court order. 3) The transfer is by a mortgagor or mortgagee incident to a foreclosure or deed in lieu of fore-closure, or is incident to a contract forfeiture. 4) A transfer from an estate, conservatorship, or trust. 5) A transfer between joint tenants or tenants in common. 6) A transfer to a spouse or a lineal descendent of the transferor. 7) A transfer between spouses as a result of a dissolution of marriage or legal separation. 8) A transfer to or from a governmental body. 9) A transfer by quit claim deed.

SELLER(S) DISCLOSURE: Seller(s) discloses the information regarding this property based on information known or reasonably available to the Seller(s). The Seller(s) has owned the property since _____. The Seller(s) certifies that as of the date signed, this information is true and accurate to the best of my/our knowledge.

Seller _____   Seller _____
Date _____   Date _____

BUYER(S) ACKNOWLEDGMENT: Buyer(s) acknowledges receipt of a copy of this Real Estate Disclosure Statement. This statement is not intended to be a warranty or to substitute for any inspection the buyer(s) may wish to obtain.

Buyer _____   Buyer _____
Date _____ Time _____   Date _____ Time _____

Rev. 1/97

DISCLOSURE OF INFORMATION AND ACKNOWLEDGMENT
LEAD-BASED PAINT AND/OR LEAD-BASED PAINT HAZARDS

Lead Warning Statement

Every purchaser of any interest in residential real property on which a residential dwelling was built prior to 1978 is notified that such property may present exposure to lead from lead-based paint that may place young children at risk of developing lead poisoning. Lead poisoning in young children may produce permanent neurological damage. Including learning disabilities, reduced intelligence quotient, behavioral problems, and impaired memory. Lead poisoning also poses a particular risk to pregnant women. The seller of any interest in residential real property is required to provide the buyer with any information on lead-based paint hazards from risk assessments or inspections in the seller's possession and notify the buyer of any known lead-based paint hazards. A risk assessment or Inspection for possible lead-based paint hazards is recommended prior to purchase.

Seller's Disclosure (initial)

_____ (a)   Presence of lead-based paint and/or lead-based paint hazards (check one below):

☐ Known lead-based paint and/or lead-based paint hazards are present in the housing (explain):
_____
_____

☐ Seller has no knowledge of lead-based paint and/or lead-based paint hazards in the housing.

_____ (b)   Records and Reports available to the seller (check one below):

☐ Seller has provided the lessee with all available records and reports pertaining to lead-based paint and/or lead-based hazards in the housing)list documents below):
_____
_____

☐ Seller has no reports or records pertaining to lead-based paint and/or lead-based paint hazards in the housing.

Purchaser's Acknowledgment (initial)

_____ (c)   Purchaser has received copies of all information listed above.

_____ (d)   Purchaser has received the pamphlet *"Protect Your Family From Lead in You Home."*

_____ (e)   Purchase has (check one below):

☐ Received a 10-day opportunity (or mutually agreed upon period) to conduct a risk assessment or inspection of the presence of lead-based paint hazards; or

☐ Waived the opportunity to conduct a risk assessment or inspection for the presence of lead-based paint and/or lead-based paint hazards.

Agent's Acknowledgment (initial)

_____ (e)   Agent has informed the seller of the seller's obligations under the Federal Residential Lead-Based Paint Hazard Reduction Act (42 U.S.C. 4582 d) and is aware of his/her responsibility to ensure compliance.

Certification of Accuracy

The following parties have reviewed the information above and certify, to the best of their knowledge, that the information provided by the signatory is true and accurate.

Seller _____ Date / /   Seller _____ Date / /

Purchaser _____ Date / /   Purchaser _____ Date / /

Agent _____ Date / /   Agent _____ Date / /

Reprinted with permission, Iowa City Area Association of REALTORS®. Endorsement not implied.

APPENDIX
E

Exclusive
Authorization
and
Right to Sell

CALIFORNIA
ASSOCIATION
OF REALTORS®

EXCLUSIVE AUTHORIZATION AND RIGHT TO SELL

1. **EXCLUSIVE RIGHT TO SELL:** _____ ("Seller") hereby employs and grants
_____ ("Broker") the exclusive and irrevocable right,
commencing on (date) _____ and expiring at 11:59 P.M. on (date) _____ ("Listing Period")
to sell or exchange the real property in the City of _____, County of _____,
California, described as: _____ ("Property").

2. **TERMS OF SALE:**
   A. **LIST PRICE:** The listing price shall be _____
   _____ ($ _____).

   B. **PERSONAL PROPERTY:** The following items of personal property are included in the above price: _____
   _____
   _____

   C. **ADDITIONAL TERMS:** _____
   _____

3. **MULTIPLE LISTING SERVICE:** Information about this listing ☐ will, ☐ will not, be provided to a multiple listing service ("MLS") of Broker's selection and all terms of the transaction, including, if applicable, financing will be provided to the MLS for publication, dissemination and use by persons and entities on terms approved by the MLS. Seller authorizes Broker to comply with all applicable MLS rules.

4. **TITLE:** Seller warrants that Seller and no other persons have title to the Property, except as follows: _____
   _____

5. **COMPENSATION TO BROKER:**
   Notice: The amount or rate of real estate commissions is not fixed by law. They are set by each Broker individually and may be negotiable between Seller and Broker.
   A. Seller agrees to pay to Broker as compensation for services irrespective of agency relationship(s), either ☐ _____ percent of the listing price (or if a sales contract is entered into, of the sales price), or ☐ $ _____,
   AND _____ as follows:
   1. If Broker, Seller, cooperating broker, or any other person, produces a buyer(s) who offers to purchase the Property on the above price and terms, or on any price and terms acceptable to Seller during the Listing Period, or any extension;
   2. If within _____ calendar days after expiration of the Listing Period or any extension, the Property is sold, conveyed, leased, or otherwise transferred to anyone with whom Broker or a cooperating broker has had negotiations, provided that Broker gives Seller, prior to or within **5 calendar days** after expiration of the Listing Period or any extension, a written notice with the name(s) of the prospective purchaser(s);
   3. If, without Broker's prior written consent, the Property is withdrawn from sale, conveyed, leased, rented, otherwise transferred, or made unmarketable by a voluntary act of Seller during the Listing Period, or any extension.
   B. If completion of the sale is prevented by a party to the transaction other than Seller, then compensation due under paragraph 5A shall be payable only if and when Seller collects damages by suit, settlement, or otherwise, and then in an amount equal to the lesser of one-half of the damages recovered or the above compensation, after first deducting title and escrow expenses and the expenses of collection, if any.

C. In addition, Seller agrees to pay: _____
_____

D. Broker is authorized to cooperate with other brokers, and divide with other brokers the above compensation in any manner acceptable to Broker;

E. Seller hereby irrevocably assigns to Broker the above compensation from Seller's funds and proceeds in escrow.

F. Seller warrants that Seller has no obligation to pay compensation to any other broker regarding the transfer of the Property except: _____
_____

If the Property is sold to anyone listed above during the time Seller is obligated to compensate another broker: (a) Broker is not entitled to compensation under this Agreement and (b) Broker is not obligated to represent Seller with respect to such transaction.

6. BROKER'S AND SELLER'S DUTIES: Broker agrees to exercise reasonable effort and due diligence to achieve the purposes of this Agreement, and is authorized to advertise and market the Property in any medium selected by Broker. Seller agrees to consider offers presented by Broker, and to act in good faith toward accomplishing the sale of the Property. Seller further agrees, regardless of responsibility, to indemnify, defend and hold Broker harmless from all claims, disputes, litigation, judgments and attorney's fees arising from any incorrect information supplied by Seller, whether contained in any document, omitted therefrom, or otherwise, or from any material facts which Seller knows but fails to disclose.

7. AGENCY RELATIONSHIPS: Broker shall act as the agent for Seller in any resulting transaction. Depending upon the circumstances, it may be necessary or appropriate for Broker to act as an agent for both Seller and buyer, exchange party, or one or more additional parties ("Buyer"). Broker shall, as soon as practicable, disclose to Seller any election to act as a dual agent representing both Seller and Buyer. If a Buyer is procured directly by Broker or an associate licensee in Broker's firm, Seller hereby consents to Broker acting as a dual agent for Seller and such Buyer. In the event of an exchange, Seller hereby consents to Broker collecting compensation from additional parties for services rendered, provided there is disclosure to all parties of such agency and compensation. Seller understands that Broker may have or obtain listings on other properties, and that potential buyers may consider, make offers on, or purchase through Broker, property the same as or similar to Seller's Property. Seller consents to Broker's representation of sellers and buyers of other properties before, during, and after the expiration of this Agreement.

8. DEPOSIT: Broker is authorized to accept and hold on Seller's behalf a deposit to be applied toward the sales price.

Seller and Broker acknowledge receipt of copy of this page, which constitutes Page 1 of _____ Pages.

Seller's Initials (_____) (_____) Broker's Initials (_____) (_____)

Published and Distributed by:
REAL ESTATE BUSINESS SERVICES, INC.
a subsidiary of the CALIFORNIA ASSOCIATION OF REALTORS®
525 South Virgil Avenue, Los Angeles, California 90020
PRINT DATE

REVISED 10/97

OFFICE USE ONLY
Reviewed by Broker
or Designee _____
Date _____

EQUAL HOUSING OPPORTUNITY

EXCLUSIVE AUTHORIZATION AND RIGHT TO SELL (A-14 PAGE 1 OF 2)

Property Address: _____

9. **LOCKBOX:**
   A. A lockbox is designed to hold a key to the Property to permit access to the Property by Broker, cooperating brokers, MLS participants, their authorized licensees and representatives, and accompanied prospective buyers.
   B. Broker, cooperating brokers, MLS and Associations/Boards of REALTORS® are **not** insurers against theft, loss, vandalism, or damage attributed to the use of a lockbox. Seller is advised to verify the existence of, or obtain, appropriate insurance through Seller's own insurance broker.
   C. (If checked:) ☐ Seller authorizes Broker to install a lockbox. If Seller does not occupy the Property, Seller shall be responsible for obtaining occupant(s)' written permission for use of a lockbox.
10. **SIGN:** (If checked:) ☐ Seller authorizes Broker to install a FOR SALE/SOLD sign on the Property.
11. **DISPUTE RESOLUTION:**
   A. **MEDIATION:** Seller and Broker agree to mediate any dispute or claim arising between them out of this Agreement, or any resulting transaction, before resorting to arbitration or court action, subject to paragraph 11C below. Mediation fees, if any, shall be divided equally among the parties involved. If any party commences an action based on a dispute or claim to which this paragraph applies, without first attempting to resolve the matter through mediation, then that party shall not be entitled to recover attorney's fees, even if they would otherwise be available to that party in any such action. THIS MEDIATION PROVISION APPLIES WHETHER OR NOT THE ARBITRATION PROVISION IS INITIALED.
   B. **ARBITRATION OF DISPUTES: Seller and Broker agree that any dispute or claim in Law or equity arising between them regarding the obligation to pay compensation under this Agreement, which is not settled through mediation, shall be decided by neutral, binding arbitration, subject to paragraph 11C below. The arbitrator shall be a retired judge or justice, or an attorney with at least five years of residential real estate experience, unless the parties mutually agree to a different arbitrator, who shall render an award in accordance with substantive California Law. In all other respects, the arbitration shall be conducted in accordance with Part III, Title 9 of the California Code of Civil Procedure. Judgment upon the award of the arbitrator(s) may be entered in any court having jurisdiction. The parties shall have the right to discovery in accordance with Code of Civil Procedure §1283.05.**

      "NOTICE: BY INITIALING IN THE SPACE BELOW YOU ARE AGREEING TO HAVE ANY DISPUTE ARISING OUT OF THE MATTERS INCLUDED IN THE 'ARBITRATION OF DISPUTES' PROVISION DECIDED BY NEUTRAL ARBITRATION AS PROVIDED BY CALIFORNIA LAW AND YOU ARE GIVING UP ANY RIGHTS YOU MIGHT POSSESS TO HAVE THE DISPUTE LITIGATED IN A COURT OR JURY TRIAL. BY INITIALING IN THE SPACE BELOW YOU ARE GIVING UP YOUR JUDICIAL RIGHTS TO DISCOVERY AND APPEAL, UNLESS THOSE RIGHTS ARE SPECIFICALLY INCLUDED IN THE 'ARBITRATION OF DISPUTES' PROVISION. IF YOU REFUSE TO SUBMIT TO ARBITRATION AFTER AGREEING TO THIS PROVISION, YOU MAY BE COMPELLED TO ARBITRATE UNDER THE AUTHORITY OF THE CALIFORNIA CODE OF CIVIL PROCEDURE. YOUR AGREEMENT TO THIS ARBITRATION PROVISION IS VOLUNTARY."

      "WE HAVE READ AND UNDERSTAND THE FOREGOING AND AGREE TO SUBMIT DISPUTES ARISING OUT OF THE MATTERS INCLUDED IN THE 'ARBITRATION OF DISPUTES' PROVISION TO NEUTRAL ARBITRATION." Seller's Initials _____/_____   Broker's Initials _____/_____
   C. **EXCLUSIONS FROM MEDIATION AND ARBITRATION:** The following matters are excluded from Mediation and Arbitration hereunder: (a) A judicial or non-judicial foreclosure or other action or proceeding to enforce a deed of trust, mortgage, or installment land sale contract as defined in Civil Code §2985; (b) An unlawful detainer action; (c) The filing or enforcement of a mechanic's lien; (d) Any matter which is within the jurisdiction of a probate, small claims, or bankruptcy court; and (e) An action for bodily injury or wrongful death, or for latent or patent defects to which Code of Civil Procedure §337.1 or §337.15 applies. The filing of a court action to enable the recording of a notice of pending action, for order of attachment, receivership, injunction, or other provisional remedies, shall not constitute a violation of the mediation and arbitration provisions.

12. **EQUAL HOUSING OPPORTUNITY:** The Property is offered in compliance with federal, state, and local anti-discrimination laws.

13. **ATTORNEY'S FEES:** In any action, proceeding, or arbitration between Seller and Broker regarding the obligation to pay compensation under this Agreement, the prevailing Seller or Broker shall be entitled to reasonable attorney's fees and costs, except as provided in paragraph 11A.

14. **ADDITIONAL TERMS:** _____
_____
_____

15. **ENTIRE CONTRACT:** All prior discussions, negotiations, and agreements between the parties concerning the subject matter of this Agreement are superseded by this Agreement, which constitutes the entire contract and a complete and exclusive expression of their agreement, and may not be contradicted by evidence of any prior agreement or contemporaneous oral agreement. This Agreement and any supplement, addendum, or modification, including any photocopy or facsimile, may be executed in counterparts.

Seller warrants that Seller is the owner of the Property or has the authority to execute this contract. Seller acknowledges that Seller has read and understands this Agreement, and has received a copy.

Seller _____ Date _____   Seller _____ Date _____

Address _____   Address _____

City _____ State _____ Zip _____   City _____ State _____ Zip _____

Real Estate Broker (Firm) _____   By (Agent) _____ Date _____

Address _____   Telephone _____

City _____ State _____ Zip _____   Fax _____

Page 2 of _____ Pages.

REVISED 10/97

OFFICE USE ONLY
Reviewed by Broker
or, Designee _____
Date _____

EQUAL HOUSING
OPPORTUNITY

EXCLUSIVE AUTHORIZATION AND RIGHT TO SELL (A-14 PAGE 2 OF 2)

Reprinted with permission, California Association of REALTORS®. Endorsement not implied.

APPENDIX

F

Contingency Supplement/ Addendum

CALIFORNIA ASSOCIATION OF REALTORS®

CONTINGENCY SUPPLEMENT/ADDENDUM
(TERMS OF CONTINGENCY, NOTICE TO REMOVE CONTINGENCY, AND REMOVAL OF CONTINGENCY)

TERMS OF CONTINGENCY

The following terms and conditions are hereby incorporated and made a part of the: ☐ Residential Purchase Agreement and Receipt for Deposit, ☐ Mobile Home Purchase Contract and Receipt for Deposit, ☐ Business Purchase Contract and Receipt for Deposit, ☐ Other _____

dated _____, 19 _____, on property known as: _____ ("Property")

in which _____ is referred to as Buyer

and _____ is referred to as Seller.

A1. **Seller has the right to continue to offer the Property for sale.**

A2. In the event Seller accepts another written offer, Seller shall deliver a written **NOTICE TO REMOVE** the following contingency(s):

_____

_____

_____

_____

_____

A3. Other requirements at time of removal: _____

_____

_____

_____

A4. **NOTICE TO REMOVE** shall be deemed delivered when personally received by Buyer or _____, who is authorized to receive it. Delivery may be in person, by mail, or facsimile. If by certified mail, delivery shall be deemed to have occurred three (3) calendar days after date of certified U.S. postal mailing receipt, even if personal receipt has not occurred.

A5. Buyer shall deliver to Seller, a written **REMOVAL OF CONTINGENCY(S)** within ☐ _____ hours or ☐ _____ calendar days from receipt of Notice to Remove. In the event Buyer fails to remove the contingency(s) and comply with the requirements in paragraph A3, within the time limit specified, the purchase contract and escrow shall terminate and the deposit shall be returned to Buyer. (Funds deposited in trust accounts or in escrow are not released automatically. Release of funds requires written agreement of the parties, judicial decision or arbitration.)

A6. The contingency(s) in paragraph A2 shall be effective until close of escrow, or the time specified in paragraph A5, or _____, whichever occurs first.

The undersigned acknowledge receipt of a copy of this page.

Date _____   Date _____

Buyer _____   Seller _____

Buyer _____   Seller _____

NOTICE TO REMOVE CONTINGENCY(S)

B1. Buyer is hereby notified that Seller has accepted a written offer conditioned upon Buyer's rights to remove the contingency(s) in paragraph A2.

B2. Buyer must remove all contingency(s) in paragraph A2 and meet the other requirements in paragraph A3 within the time specified in paragraph A5. In the event Buyer fails to remove the contingency(s) and comply with the requirements in paragraph A3, within the time limit specified, the purchase contract and escrow shall terminate and the deposit shall be returned to Buyer. (Funds deposited in trust accounts or in escrow are not released automatically. Release of funds requires written agreement of the parties, judicial decision or arbitration.)

Date _____   Seller _____

                                          Seller _____

Receipt of this notice on _____ 19___ at _____ AM/PM by Buyer _____ or person authorized by Buyer
to receive it _____ is acknowledged.
            Initials   Initials

REMOVAL OF CONTINGENCY

C1. Buyer removes all of the contingencies in paragraph A2 and has satisfied the requirements to be met by Buyer under paragraph A3.

Date _____   Buyer _____

Time _____   Buyer _____

RECEIPT BY SELLER

Receipt of a copy of the above Removal of Contingency(s) is hereby acknowledged.

Date _____   Seller _____

Time _____   Seller _____

Published and Distributed by:
REAL ESTATE BUSINESS SERVICES, INC.
a subsidiary of the CALIFORNIA ASSOCIATION OF REALTORS®
525 South Virgil Avenue, Los Angeles, California 90020

┌─ OFFICE USE ONLY ─┐
Reviewed by Broker
or Designee _____
Date _____

FORM CS-14 REVISED 1992

Reprinted with permission, California Association of REALTORS®. Endorsement not implied.

APPENDIX
G

Contingency Removal

CALIFORNIA
ASSOCIATION
OF REALTORS®

CONTINGENCY REMOVAL

In accordance with the terms and conditions of the: ☐ Residential Purchase Agreement, ☐ Residential Income

Property Purchase Agreement, ☐ Vacant Land Purchase Contract, ☐ Commercial Real Estate Purchase Contract,

☐ Manufactured Home Purchase Contract, ☐ Business Purchase Contract, OR ☐ Other _____,

_____

("Agreement"), dated _____, on property known as: _____

_____ ("Property"),

in which _____ is referred to as Buyer,

and _____ is referred to as Seller,

the undersigned ☐ Buyer, ☐ Seller, removes the following contingency(s): _____

_____

_____

_____

And represents that the following additional requirements, if any, have been satisfied: _____

_____

_____

The person removing the contingency agrees to purchase/sell the Property in accordance with all other terms and

conditions of the Agreement. The person removing the contingency has read and acknowledges receipt of a copy of this

Contingency Removal.

Dated: _____   _____
                                        (Person removing the contingency)

                                        _____
                                        (Person removing the contingency)

RECEIPT

☐ Buyer, ☐ Seller, has read and acknowledges receipt of a copy of this Contingency Removal.

Dated: _____   _____

                                          _____

Published and Distributed by:
REAL ESTATE BUSINESS SERVICES, INC.
a subsidiary of the *CALIFORNIA ASSOCIATION OF REALTORS®*
525 South Virgil Avenue, Los Angeles, California 90020

PRINT DATE

REVISED 4/98

┌─ OFFICE USE ONLY ─┐
Reviewed by Broker
or Designee _____
Date _____

EQUAL HOUSING OPPORTUNITY

CONTINGENCY REMOVAL (CR-11)

APPENDIX

H

Uniform
Settlement
Statement

HUD-1 (OMB # 2502-0265)   **HUD-1 UNIFORM SETTLEMENT STATEMENT**   Page-1

A. U.S. DEPARTMENT OF HOUSING AND URBAN DEVELOPMENT		**SETTLEMENT STATEMENT**

B. TYPE OF LOAN 1.[] FHA 2.[] FmHA 3.[] CONV. UNINS. 4.[] VA 5.[] CONV. INS.	6. File Number:	7. Loan Number
	8. Mortgage Insurance Case Number:	

C. NOTE: This form furnishes a statement of settlement costs. Amounts paid to and by the settlement agent are shown. Items marked "(p.o.c.)" were paid outside the closing; they are shown for informational purposes and are not included in the totals.
NOTE: TIN=Taxpayer's Identification Number.

D. NAME & ADDRESS OF BORROWER:	E. NAME, ADDRESS & TIN OF SELLER:	F. NAME AND ADDRESS OF LENDER:
Name:	Name:	
Street:	Street:	
City:	City:	H. SETTLEMENT AGENT: NAME, ADD. & TIN
St&Zip:	St. & Zip:	
	Transferor's Identification Number:	
G. PROPERTY LOCATION:	PLACE OF SETTLEMENT:	I. SETTLEMENT DATE:

J. SUMMARY OF BORROWER'S TRANSACTION		K. SUMMARY OF SELLER'S TRANSACTION	
100. GROSS AMOUNT DUE FROM BORROWER:		**400. GROSS AMOUNT DUE TO SELLER:**	
101. Contract sales price		401. Contract sales price	
102. Personal Property		402. Personal Property	
103. Borrower's settlement charges (line 1400)	0.00	403.	
104.		404.	
105.		405.	
Adjustments for items paid by seller in advance		Adjustments for items paid by seller in advance	
106. City/town taxes to		406. City/town taxes to	
107. County taxes to		407. County taxes to	
108. Assessments to		408. Assessments to	
109.		409.	
110.		410.	
111.		411.	
112.		412.	
113.		413.	
120. GROSS AMOUNT DUE FROM BORROWER	0.00	420. GROSS AMOUNT DUE TO SELLER	0.00

200. AMOUNTS PAID BY OR IN BEHALF OF BORROWER:		500. REDUCTIONS IN AMOUNT DUE TO SELLER:	
201. Deposits or earnest money		501. Excess deposit (see instructions)	
202. Principal amount of new loan(s)		502. Settlement charges to seller (line 1400)	0.00
203. Existing loan(s) taken subject to		503. Existing loan(s) taken subject to	
204.		504. Payoff of first mortgage loan	
205.		505. Payoff of second mortgage loan	
206.		506.	
207.		507.	
208.		508.	
209.		509.	
Adjustments for items unpaid by seller		Adjustments for items unpaid by seller	
210. City/town taxes to		510. City/town taxes to	
211. County taxes to		511. County taxes to	
212. Assessments to		512. Assessments to	
213.		513.	
214.		514.	
215.		515.	
216.		516.	
217.		517.	
218.		518.	
219.		519.	
220. TOTAL PAID BY/FOR BORROWER	0.00	520. TOTAL REDUCTION AMOUNT DUE SELLER	0.00

300. CASH AT SETTLEMENT FROM/TO BORROWER		600. CASH AT SETTLEMENT TO/FROM SELLER	
301. Gross amount due from borrower (line 120)	0.00	601. Gross amount due to seller (line 420)	0.00
302. Less amounts paid by/for borrower (line 220)	0.00	602. Less reductions in amount due seller (line 520)	0.00
303. CASH [] FROM [] TO BORROWER	0.00	603. CASH [] TO [] FROM SELLER	0.00

L. SETTLEMENT CHARGES

			PAID FROM BORROWER'S FUNDS AT SETTLEMENT	PAID FROM SELLERS FUNDS AT SETTLEMENT
700. Total Sales/Broker's Commission based on price $		@ %		
Division of Commission (line 700) as follows:				
701.$	to			
702.$	to			
703. Commission paid at Settlement				0.00
704.				
800. ITEMS PAYABLE IN CONNECTION WITH LOAN				
801. Loan Origination Fee				
802. Loan Discount				
803. Appraisal Fee				
804. Credit Report				
805. Lender's Inspection Fee				
806. Mortgage Insurance Application Fee to				
807. Assumption Fee				
808.				
809.				
810.				
811.				
900. ITEMS REQUIRED BY LENDER TO BE PAID IN ADVANCE				
901. Interest				
902. Mortgage Insurance Premium				
903. Hazard Insurance Premium				
904.				
1000. RESERVES DEPOSITED WITH LENDER				
1001. Hazard insurance	months @ $	per month	0.00	///////////////
1002. Mortgage insurance	months @ $	per month	0.00	///////////////
1003. City property taxes	months @ $	per month	0.00	///////////////
1004. County property taxes	months @ $	per month	0.00	///////////////
1005. Annual assessments	months @ $	per month	0.00	///////////////
1006.				
1007.				
1008.				

1100. **TITLE CHARGES**				
1101. Settlement/closing fee	to			
1102. Abstract/title search	to			
1103. Title examination	to			
1104. Title insurance binder	to			
1105. Document preparation	to			
1106. Notary fees	to			
1107. Attorney's fees	to			
(includes above item numbers			/////////////////////////////////////	
1108. Title insurance	to			
(includes above item numbers		)		
1109. Lender's coverage	$			
1110. Owner's coverage	$			
1111.				
1112.				
1113.				
1200. **GOVERNMENT RECORDING AND TRANSFER CHARGES**				
1201. Recording fees:	Deed $	Mortgage $	Release $	
1202. City/county tax/stamps:	Deed $	Mortgage $		
1203. State tax/stamps:	Deed $	Mortgage $		
1204.				
1205.				
1300. **ADDITIONAL SETTLEMENT CHARGES**				
1301. Survey	to			
1302. Pest Inspection	to			
1303.				
1304.				
1305.				
1400. TOTAL SETTLEMENT CHARGES (this number transfers to lines 103 & 502 above)			0.00	0.00

CERTIFICATION

I have carefully reviewed the HUD-1 Settlement Statement and to the best of my knowledge and belief, it is a true and accurate statement of all receipts and disbursements made on my account or by me in this transaction. I further certify that I have received a copy of the HUD-1 Settlement Statement.

_____Seller   _____ Borrower

_____Seller   _____ Borrower

To the best of my knowledge the HUD-1 Settlement Statement which I have prepared is true and accurate account of the funds which were received and have been or will be disbursed by the undersigned as part of the settlement of this transaction.

_____Settlement Agent _____Date

WARNING: It is a crime to knowingly make false statements to the United States on this or any other similar form. Penalties upon conviction can include a fine and imprisonment. For details see: Title 18 U.S. Code Section 1001 and Section 1010.

GLOSSARY

abstract of title: The condensed history of a title to a particular piece of real estate and a certification by the abstractor that the history is complete and accurate.

accrued items: On a closing statement, items of expense that are incurred but not yet payable such as interest on a mortgage loan or taxes on real property.

affidavit of title: A written statement, made under oath by a seller or grantor of real property and acknowledged by a notary public, in which the grantor (1) identifies himself or herself and indicates marital status; (2) certifies that since the examination of the title on the date of the contracts no defects have occurred in the title; and (3) certifies that he or she is in possession of the property (if applicable).

agency: The relationship between a principal (seller or buyer) and an agent (broker-age firm and salesperson) wherein the agent is authorized to represent the principal in certain transactions such as marketing the home.

agent: One who acts or has the power to act for another. A fiduciary relationship is created when a property owner, as the principal, executes a listing agreement authorizing a licensed real estate broker to be his or her agent.

antitrust laws: Laws designed to preserve the free enterprise of the open market-place and encourage competition. Most violations of antitrust laws in the real estate business involve either price-fixing (brokers conspiring to set fixed compensation rates) or allocation of customers or markets (brokers agreeing to limit their areas of trade to certain locational boundaries).

appraisal: An estimate of the quantity, quality or value of something. The process through which conclusions of property value are obtained; also refers to the report that sets forth the estimation and conclusion of value.

appreciation: An increase in the worth or value of a property due to economic or related causes, which may prove to be either temporary or permanent; opposite of depreciation.

attorney's opinion of title: A certification by an attorney that he or she has examined an abstract of the title and has determined it to be, in his or her opinion, an accurate statement of the facts concerning the property ownership.

basis: The financial interest that the Internal Revenue Service attributes to an owner of a property for the purpose of determining annual depreciation and gain or loss on the sale of the asset. If a property was acquired by purchase, the owner's basis is the cost of the property plus the value of any capital expenditures for improvements to the property, minus any depreciation allowable or actually taken. This new basis is called the *adjusted basis.*

broker: One who acts on behalf of others for a fee or commission.

brokerage: The bringing together of parties (such as buyers and sellers) who are interested in making a real estate transaction.

capital gain: Profit earned from the sale of a property.

certificate of title: A statement of opinion on the status of the title to a parcel of real property based on an examination of public records.

closing statement: A detailed cash accounting of a real estate transaction showing all cash received, all charges and credits made, and all cash paid out in the transaction.

coinsurance clause: A clause in insurance policies covering real property that requires the policyholder to maintain fire insurance coverage generally equal to at least 80 percent of the property's actual replacement cost.

commission: Payment to a broker for services rendered such as in the sale or purchase of real property; usually a percentage of the selling price of the property.

comparables: Properties used in an appraisal report or agent's competitive market analysis that are substantially equivalent to the subject property. Similarities would include location, style, square feet, and amenities.

comparative market analysis (CMA): A comparison of the prices of recently sold homes and current comparable homes that are similar to a seller's home in terms of location, style, and amenities.

contingency: A provision in a purchase agreement that requires a certain act to be done or a certain event to occur before the agreement becomes binding. A buyer may have to secure a mortgage or a seller may have to find a home of his or her choice.

contract: A legally enforceable promise or set of promises that must be performed and for which, if a breach of the promise occurs, the law provides a remedy (such as those promises agreed to between buyer and seller in a purchase agreement).

conventional loan: A loan that requires no insurance or guarantee, as contrasted with an FHA-insured or VHA-guaranteed loan.

conveyance: A term used to refer to any document that transfers title to real property. The term is also used in describing the act of transferring.

counteroffer: A new offer made (usually by the seller) in response to an offer received from a buyer. It has the effect of rejecting the original offer, which cannot be accepted thereafter unless brought back to life by the offeror (the buyer).

credit: On a closing statement, an amount entered in a person's favor—either an amount the party has paid or an amount for which the party must be reimbursed.

debit: On a closing statement, an amount charged; that is, an amount that the debited party must pay.

default: The nonperformance of a duty under a contract; failure to meet an obligation when due. Any violation of the terms of an agreement.

discount point: A unit of measurement used for various loan charges; one point equals 1 percent of the amount of the loan.

documentary stamps/transfer tax: Tax stamps required to be affixed to a deed by state and/or local law. Often paid by the seller when the deed is recorded.

dual agency: Representing both parties to a transaction. It is illegal in many states and in others must first be agreed to by both parties.

earnest money: Money deposited by a buyer under the terms of a purchase agreement, to be forfeited if the buyer defaults but applied to the purchase price if the sale is closed. It accompanies a written purchase agreement.

encumbrance: A right or interest that someone else holds in a homeowner's property such as a mortgage, tax, or judgment lien; an easement or restriction on the use of the land that may reduce the value or use of a property.

equity: The interest or value that an owner has in property over and above what he or she owes on a mortgage.

escrow: The closing of a transaction through a third party called an escrow agent, or escrowee, who receives funds and documents to be delivered upon the performance of certain conditions outlined in the escrow conditions.

evidence of title: Proof of ownership of property; commonly a certificate of title, an abstract of title with lawyer's opinion, title insurance, or a Torrens registration certificate.

exclusive agency listing: A listing contract under which the owner appoints a real estate broker as the exclusive agent for a designated period of time to sell the property, on the owner's stated terms, for a commission. The owner reserves the right to sell without paying anyone a commission if he or she sells to a prospect who has not been introduced or claimed by the broker.

Fair Housing Act: The federal law that prohibits discrimination in housing based on race, color, religion, sex, handicap, familial status, and national origin.

FHA loan: A loan insured by the Federal Housing Authority and made by an approved lender in accordance with FHA regulations. It is a government loan often requiring discount points that are often paid by the seller.

fiduciary: One in whom trust and confidence is placed; a reference to a broker employed under the terms of a listing contract or buyer agency agreement.

fiduciary relationship: A relationship of trust and confidence, as between attorney and client or principal and agent (seller and broker).

FSBO: A property for sale but not listed with a brokerage firm but rather For Sale By Owner.

grantor: The person transferring title to or an interest in real property to a grantee. Usually the seller, but could be the executor of an estate or the parent "giving" a farm to a child.

home equity loan: A loan (sometimes called a line of credit) under which a property owner uses his or her residence as collateral and can then draw funds up to a pre-arranged amount against the property. The owner is borrowing against the equity on the home.

homeowners insurance policy: A standardized package insurance policy that covers a residential real estate owner against financial loss in the event of fire, theft, public liability, and other common risks. It is usually a lender requirement and a good protection.

listing agreement: A contract between an owner (as principal) and a real estate broker (as agent) by which the broker is employed by the owner as agent to find a buyer for the owner's real estate on the owner's terms. The owner then agrees to pay a commission to the broker when the party sells and closes.

listing broker: The broker in a multiple listing situation from whose office a listing agreement is initiated, as opposed to the cooperating broker, from whose office negotiations leading up to a sale are initiated. The listing broker and the cooperating broker may be the same person if the listing broker also has the buyer.

market value: The most probable price property would bring in an arm's-length (objective) transaction under normal conditions on the open market.

mortgage: A conditional transfer or pledge of real estate as security for the payment of a debt. Also the document creating a mortgage lien.

multiple listing service (MLS): A marketing organization composed of member brokers who cooperate to share their inventory of properties in the hope of procuring a larger number of ready, willing, and able buyers more quickly than they could on their own. Most multiple listing services accept exclusive right to sell or exclusive agency listings from their member brokers.

net listing: A listing based on a specific sum or the net price the seller will receive if the property is sold. The broker can offer the property for sale at a higher price obtainable to increase the commission. This type of listing is illegal in many states because it is so open to abuses.

offer and acceptance: Two essential components of a valid contract; a "meeting of the minds." An agreement by a buyer and a seller on the provision of the purchase agreement.

open listing: A listing contract under which the broker's commission is contingent on the broker's producing a ready, willing, and able buyer before the property is sold by the seller or another broker. The seller pays a commission only to the broker who sells the property. If the owner sells the property himself or herself, a commission is due to no one.

principal: (1) A sum loaned to a purchaser of a home in a mortgage note; (2) the original amount (as in a loan) of the total due and payable at a certain date; (3) a main party to a transaction—the person for whom the agent works—usually a buyer or a seller.

prorations: Expenses, either prepaid or paid in arrears, that are divided between buyer and seller at the closing. Property taxes are typically prorated at closing.

protected class: Any group of people designated as such by the Department of Housing and Urban Development (HUD) in consideration of federal and state civil rights legislation. Currently includes ethnic minorities, women, religious groups, the disabled, and others.

real estate: Land; a portion of the earth's surface extending downward to the center of the earth and upward infinitely into space, including all things attached permanently to it, whether naturally or artificially.

real property: The interests, benefits, and rights inherent in real estate ownership such as the right to be in possession and the right to exclude persons from entering.

Realtists: A term reserved solely for the use of active members affiliated with the National Association of Real Estate Brokers.

REALTOR® A registered trademark reserved for the sole use of active members of local REALTOR® boards affiliated with the National Association of Realtors.

recording: The act of entering or recording documents affecting or conveying interests in real estate in the recorder's office in each county (usually housed in the courthouse).

salesperson: A person who performs real estate activities while employed by or associated with a licensed real estate broker. An agent of the broker. Considered to be an agent by a buyer or a seller.

subagent: One who is employed by a person already acting as an agent. Typically a reference to a salesperson licensed under a broker (agent) who is employed under the terms of a listing agreement, but could be another brokerage firm who elects to procure the buyer but represents the seller.

time is of the essence: A phrase in a contract that requires the performance of a certain act with a stated period of time or the contract can be voided.

title: (1) The right to ownership of the land; (2) the evidence of ownership of land such as a deed for the property.

title insurance: A policy insuring the owner or mortgagee against loss by reason of defects in the title to a parcel of real estate, other than encumbrances, defects, and matters specifically excluded by the policy.

title search: The examination of public records relating to real estate to determine the current state of the ownership.

Torrens system: A method of evidencing title by registration with the proper public authority, generally called the registrar, named for its founder, Sir Robert Torrens.

VA loan: A mortgage loan on approved property made to a qualified veteran by an authorized lender and approved by the Department of Veteran Affairs to limit the lender's possible loss. A government loan that often requires discount points to be paid by the buyer or the seller.

RESOURCES

Books and Pamphlets

Dress Your House for Success. Martha Webb and Sarah Parsons Zackheim (Crown, 1997).

The E-Z Legal Forms to Buying/Selling Your Home: Do-it-Yourself Kit (E-Z Legal, 1997).

How to List and Sell Real Estate in the 21st Century. Danielle Kennedy and Warren Jamison (Prentice-Hall, 1999).

How to Sell Your Home Fast, for the Highest Price, in Any Market: From A Real Estate Expert Who Knows All the Tricks. Terry Eilers (Hyperion, 1997).

Kiplinger's Buying & Selling A Home. Kiplinger's Personal Finance Magazine (Kiplinger Books, 1993).

Modern Real Estate Practices (14th edition). Fillmore W. Galaty, Wellington J. Allaway, and Robert C. Kyle (Real Estate Education Company, a division of Dearborn Financial Publishing, 1996).

Principles of Real Estate Practice. Stephen Mettling and David Cusic (Performance Publishing Company, 1996).

The Future Consumer. Frank Feather (Warwick Publishing, 1994).

Packaging Your Home for Profit. Bruce Percelay and Peter Arnold (Little, Brown).

Sell Your Property Fast: How to Take Back a Mortgage without being Taken! Bill Broadbent and George Rosenberg (Who's Who in Creative Real Estate, Ventura, CA, 800-729-5147).

Stephen Pollan's Foolproof Guide to Selling Your Home. Stephen Pollan and Mark Levine (Simon & Schuster, 1996).

The 201 Questions Every Homebuyer and Homeseller Must Ask! Edith Lank (Dearborn Financial Publishing, 1996).

Home Buyer's and Seller's Guide to Radon. Environmental Protection Agency. (Public Information Center, 401 M St., SW, Washington, DC 20460. Stock # 055-000-00428-5.)

Magazines

Kiplinger's Personal Finance Magazine. The Kiplinger Washington Editors, Inc., 1729 H St., NW, Washington, DC 20006.

Real Estate Business. Real Estate Brokerage Managers Council and Real Estate Residential Sales Council, 430 North Michigan Avenue, Suite 300, Chicago, IL 60611-4092.

Videos

Dress Your House for Success. David Knox Seminars, 11021 Mt. Curve Rd., Eden Prarie, MN 55343, 800-533-4494.

Pricing Your Home to Sell. David Knox Seminars, 11021 Mt. Curve Rd., Eden Prarie, MN 55343, 800-533-4494.

The Real Estate Report: The Seller's Role. Rick Willis. Excellence in Action, Inc., P.O. Box 1233, Ellicott City, MD 21041.

Successful Selling. John Grogan. Marketing Systems for Today Corporation, 5726 Southwyck Blvd., Toledo, OH 43614.

What Every Seller Should Know about Home Inspections. Housemaster 800-526-3939 or Ron Reem 888-344-9665.

Audio

Negotiating in the Best Interest of the Client. Roger Turcotte. Roger Turcotte & Co., P.O. Box 806, Contoocook, NH 03229. 603-746-5705.

Online Resources

General

Homefair, http://www.homefair.com/
  Provides information on selling and buying a house. Includes advice on
  how to pick the best mortagage and how to organize your move.

Home Seller's Information Center, http://www.ourfamilyplace.com/
  homeseller/
  Offers tips on pricing your home; working with an agent or going
  FSBO; and preparing your house to be shown.

Court TV's Legal Cafe,http://www.courttv.com/lealcafe/home/selling1/
  sellhome_background.html
  Learn about about the right time to sell your home, how to work with
  real estate agents, the nitty-gritty of contracts and disclosures, and tax
  issues.

For Marketing FSBO Properties

Sell Your Home Yourself, Do It Yourself Real Estate,
  http://www.sellyourhomeyourself.com/

FSBO USA, http://fsbo-usa.com/

FSBO Marketer, http://www.fsbormart.com/

For Sale By Owner Network, http://www.f-s-b-o.com/

By Owner Online, http://www.by-owner-ol.com/

INDEX